A Perfect Trip to Italy—
in the Golden Years

VOLUME 1:

Florence, Venice,

Rome, and Tuscany

Sharon Wilson

iUniverse, Inc.
Bloomington

A Perfect Trip to Italy—in the Golden Years
Volume 1: Florence, Venice, Rome, and Tuscany

iUniverse books may be ordered through booksellers or by contacting:

iUniverse
1663 Liberty Drive
Bloomington, IN 47403
www.iuniverse.com
1-800-Authors (1-800-288-4677)

ISBN: 978-1-4502-8443-1 (pbk)
ISBN: 978-1-4502-8441-7 (cloth)
ISBN: 978-1-4502-8442-4 (ebk)

Library of Congress Control Number: 2011900245

Printed in the United States of America

iUniverse rev. date: 1/15/2011

Contents

Acknowledgements-Grazie

In order to write this book, I needed the encouragement and assistance of friends and family. To write a book, I think one must be in love with the subject. I enjoyed the many hours required for research and writing because I love Italy. The kindness and generosity of the Italian people contributed enormously to this book. The Italian people welcome anyone who loves their country. They share their language, culture, music, art, and recipes to anyone who is interested.

I appreciate my Italian teacher, Amelia Ippoliti, for her generosity and humor. She has taught the language, history, and culture of her country to me for the past three years.

I appreciate my neighbor, Marianne Nimeshein, who told me to go work on my book every day.

I appreciate my friends who love Italy as much as I do (especially Barbara Sehorn and Tarry Pesola).

I appreciate my friend, Melba Davis, for contributing many of the photos used in this book.

I appreciate my friend, Marsha Enrici, for her editing skills.

I appreciate many of my friends who are eagerly waiting to read my book.

I appreciate my country, the United States of America, for giving me the freedom to travel wherever I want.

INTRODUCTION

When retirees decide to travel in their Golden Years, most people sign up for a tour where everything is planned for them, including airline tickets, hotels, meals, and sightseeing. What they do not know is that there are many advantages to traveling without a tour guide and a set itinerary. I wrote this book to assist those in the Golden Years who want to make travel a real adventure without worrying about where they will sleep, eat, or catch the next bus or train. I also wrote this book to show that travel is possible even when your bones are aching and your muscles are stiff. I traveled to Italy when I was twenty-five years old and when I was sixty-five years old. There is a big difference! At twenty-five I could sleep on trains and even on train station benches. At sixty-five, if I sleep on anything but a comfortable bed, I will not be able to walk the next day. In the Golden Years, you may want to spend a day resting in your apartment or just sitting in a piazza as you watch people strolling down the cobblestone streets. Just think how nice it would be to come home for a nap, have a cup of tea, or put your feet up and listen to some beautiful music after visiting a famous art museum or cathedral. This book is also useful for those not in the Golden Years. I know many in their thirties and forties who have bad knees and backs. By reading this travel book, I hope that many of you will learn that you can travel at your own pace and decide what activities are best for you.

Now, let us get down to specifics. Have you been to Italy? It is one of the most interesting and beautiful countries outside of the United States. My first trip to Italy was in 1972. I carried a backpack and used Frommer's *Europe on $5 a Day* book. Things have changed. Now, I do not even like to carry a heavy purse, and it is difficult to find a *panini* (sandwich) for less than $5! However, I am now retired, and I finally have the time to travel again. During my first few months of retirement, I had a serious attack of sciatica, and I could barely walk. The MRI test revealed that I had spinal stenosis and bulging discs. After finding a wonderful spinal specialist and undergoing shots of Kenalog, I was so happy to walk again. I knew I would not be able to travel the way I did back in the 70's, but I had dreamed for many years of the time when I could return to Italy. After a year of research, I planned a trip that would take into consideration that I am now 65 instead of 25. It worked! On what I call a "perfect trip," I traveled throughout Italy for a month and discovered that age and arthritis are not obstacles.

Many think of all the obstacles to traveling on your own: not knowing how to communicate in a foreign language, how to plan for medical emergencies, how to exchange money, how to get where you are going, how to find a great place to stay, what to see, and even how to find a restroom. In the Golden Years, you also have to deal with physical obstacles like climbing stairs, walking long distances, and fatigue. In the following chapters, you will find out how to remove all of these obstacles in a detailed and easy to understand format. Some may even want to customize their own trip after reading this book to satisfy particular interests and desires. By reading this book, you will find that you can travel to Italy with your spouse, friends, relatives, or even alone and feel totally free to do whatever you want and have the time of your life. I will provide every detail that you need for a perfect trip to Italy (*un perfetto viaggio in Italia*). In addition, you will also find that you will save a lot of money. In fact, you can travel to Italy for a month on your own for less than you would spend on a ten-day tour.

I like to use Florence as a base because of its central location with very good connections to many other cities. In this book, we will travel from Florence to Rome, Venice, and Milan. By train, Venice is two and a half hours away, Rome is one and a half hours away, and Milan is two and a half hours away. You can take many day trips from Florence. You can take a train or bus in the morning to visit places like Siena, Portofino, and Lucca and return home to your comfortable bed before dark that night.

You will have experiences in Italy that no tour would provide. For example, you can sleep as late as you want. You will not have to meet your tour group at 6 AM. You can also eat when you feel like eating. Most important, you will be able to determine how many steps you want to take in a day. My research uncovered elevators and ways to reach many places without straining the back. You will also be able to sit down and rest whenever your aches and pains become unbearable. You can return to your room whenever you want to take a nap.

I wrote this book, *A Perfect Trip to Italy in the Golden Years*, to provide the kind of information you need to travel to Italy comfortably on your own. When I planned my first trip to Italy, I had to research many books and Web sites to prepare for a trip. My personal experiences of travel in Italy provide you with the details needed to enjoy your travel experience. There were no comprehensive travel guidebooks available that took age and physical limitations into consideration. I am happy to share what I have learned so that you will have a wonderful time in a wonderful country.

In the following chapters, I provide detailed information on how to travel to Italy. Being well prepared will enable you to relax and enjoy the Italy's many wonders. I provide detailed instructions on visiting the most popular and beautiful cities of Florence, Venice, and Rome. I will also show you how to travel to the many charming little towns in Tuscany. Usually a travel guidebook will tell you about the important sites to visit, but they do not tell you how many steps you must climb or how many blocks, or miles, you must walk. In your Golden Years, you do not have to see everything. There are so many beautiful sights in Italy that you can pick and choose the ones that accommodate your physical condition. This is the time of your life when you should take advantage of ferries, limos, and taxis. For example, I did not have to hike the trails of the Cinque Terra hanging on to narrow bridges and climbing across rocky terrain to see the beautiful villages of pink and yellow ancient villages. I took a ferry and actually had a better view of the beautiful terrain.

CHAPTER 1:
Choosing the Right Travel Companions

If you are married, you might not have the choice of a travel companion! On the other hand, choosing travel companions is one of the most important things in planning your trip. When you travel with someone, you really get to know that person at a much deeper level than socializing at a party or going out to lunch with a friend. In the Golden Years, people are often set in their ways and less flexible. Here, I will discuss some important factors in choosing a travel companion. It is not necessary to choose someone just like you, but there is much to be said about compatibility. No matter what you do, there is a lot of walking. However, when you are traveling at your own speed, you can sit down on a bench or rest for a few minutes without losing the group. It is not a good idea to choose a travel companion who wants to get some place in record time!

When you plan your own trip, you can choose your travel companions. When you travel on a tour, you often do not get to choose with whom who you are traveling. Most people are courteous and considerate, but one rude or obnoxious person can ruin your trip.

Through my experience as a counselor, therapist, and teacher in the field of interpersonal relationships, I have learned that the people with whom we associate can determine the enjoyment of our experiences. I have also learned that I can positively or negatively affect the enjoyment of the experiences of others.

Personality

I have included some information about factors of personality that can be used in having discussions with your potential travel companions. Most adults have some idea of where they fall on the following continua of personality factors. According to Saucier and Goldberg in *The Language of Personality*, the five-factor model of personality provides a conceptual framework for integrating all of the research findings and theory in personality psychology. Where you fall on these continua does not mean you are good or bad. It just explains individual differences in personality. I have summarized the five factors of personality and their constituent traits as follows:

Openness

A person who is open appreciates art, emotion, and adventure. The open person enjoys unusual ideas and likes a variety of experience. Those who are high in openness are imaginative and intellectually curious. They tend to be more aware of their feelings, and they are willing to share what they are thinking and feeling.

Those who are low in openness are usually down-to-earth and conventional. They tend to have traditional interests. They prefer the plain, straightforward, and obvious over the complex, ambiguous, and subtle. They may find the arts and sciences boring and uninteresting.

Conscientiousness

The highly conscientious person shows self-discipline, acts responsibly, and aims for achievement. The conscientious prefer planned rather than spontaneous activity. There are many benefits of high conscientiousness. Conscientious individuals avoid trouble and achieve high levels of success through purposeful planning and persistence. They are also positively regarded by others as intelligent and reliable. On the negative side, they can be compulsive perfectionists or workaholics.

People with very low conscientiousness are often perceived as lazy, irresponsible, and impulsive. This is because they prefer to live for the moment. They have the ability to take things as they come and accept problems as normal occurrences.

Traveling well does take a lot of planning. If one companion is willing to follow along without taking responsibility for some of the adventures, the conscientious person may feel taken advantage of and the low conscientious person may feel "bossed." No one likes to feel demeaned or to be treated like a careless child. Whether you are high or low in conscientiousness, it is important to show respect for your travel companion.

Introversion-Extroversion

A person high in extroversion exhibits high energy and tends to seek stimulation in the company of others. They tend to be enthusiastic, action-oriented individuals who are likely to say "Yes!" or "Let's go!" to opportunities for excitement. In groups, they like to talk, assert themselves, and draw attention to themselves.

Introverts lack the exuberance, energy, and activity levels of extroverts. They tend to be quiet, low-key, deliberate, and less involved in the social world. Their lack of social involvement should not be interpreted as shyness or depression. Introverts simply need less stimulation and desire more time alone than extraverts.

If you are an extrovert, just dying to socialize and ready to go to the next activity, you may feel frustrated with an introvert who would rather sit in the apartment and read a book or who would rather sleep on the train than have a conversation. If you are an introvert, an extrovert may overwhelm you.

Agreeableness

Agreeableness is a tendency to be compassionate and cooperative rather than suspicious and antagonistic towards others. Agreeable individuals value getting along with others and have a real concern for social harmony. They are generally considerate, friendly, generous, helpful, and willing to compromise their interests with others. Agreeable people also have an optimistic view of human nature. They believe people are basically honest, decent, and trustworthy.

Disagreeable individuals place self-interest above getting along with others. They do not like to be told what to do. They are generally unconcerned with others' well-being, and they are less likely to extend themselves for other people. Sometimes their skepticism about others' motives causes them to be suspicious, unfriendly, and uncooperative. Being a team player is important when traveling with one or more travel companions. For example, you may not want to participate in cooking an inexpensive meal at home, but you do anyway just to be part of the team.

Neuroticism

Neuroticism is the tendency to experience negative emotions, such as anger, anxiety, or depression. It is sometimes called emotional instability. Those who score high in neuroticism are emotionally reactive and vulnerable to stress. They are more likely to interpret ordinary situations as threatening. They view minor frustrations as hopelessly difficult. Their negative emotional reactions tend to persist for unusually long periods of time. This means they are often in a bad mood. Those with neurotic tendencies have a hard time making decisions and coping with stress.

At the other end of the scale, individuals who score low in neuroticism are less easily upset and are less emotionally reactive. They tend to be calm, emotionally stable, and free from persistent negative feelings. Freedom from negative feelings does not mean that low scorers experience a lot of positive feelings. Frequency of positive emotions is a component of the extraversion domain. One example of high neuroticism is the "get my own way" syndrome, when a person becomes moody, untalkative, and resentful if not allowed to do what he or she wants. It is always important to negotiate with friends so that everyone gets what they want sometimes even if at different times. For example, I may want to go to a particular restaurant when others do not. Through negotiation I can get what I want, going to a particular restaurant, but on a different day. There is no need to get bent out of shape over a meal!

Attitude Toward Life

Besides the five factors of personality, a person has other personal characteristics that determine attitude and behavior. There are two main attitudes toward life in general: positive and negative. As we have learned in our elementary science classes, positives and negatives attract. However, when choosing a travel companion, for some strange reason, this principle does not work. Someone who has a positive attitude in life, thinking that most things will turn out well, can be worn down by someone with a negative attitude who is always worrying that something bad will happen. On the other hand, someone with a generally negative attitude will feel overwhelmed by someone who thinks that anything bad will soon turn to good. Therefore, it is important to know your possible travel companion well enough to know whether that person has a basic negative or basic positive attitude.

Values

Although we cannot see or touch our values, they are every bit as real as any physical object. People may dedicate their entire lives or even give up their lives to pursue their values, as so many loyal patriots have done by fighting for the values of freedom, equality, and human rights.

We all have values that determine our decisions and guide our lives. Those who value their individuality take responsibility, act self-reliantly, and behave with self-respect. Those who value truthfulness cannot bring themselves to tell a lie. Those who value family or friendship sacrifice their personal interests for the good of others. Those who value goodness cannot bring themselves to do something that they know is wrong. Some other common values are loyalty, reliability, honesty, generosity, and trustworthiness. Values guide us to take responsibility for family, friends, community, or country. On a more physical level, we may place great value on cleanliness, punctuality, orderliness, accuracy, and physical perfection in whatever we do.

Values determine our political views. Although politics may not come up when you are traveling, a person with extreme political views may cause discomfort in others.

We express values in our relationships with other people. The quality of your travel experience increases if your companions share similar values.

Interests

It is fun to share similar interests when traveling, but a travel companion with different interests could make your adventure more interesting. For example, if someone is interested in architecture, you might learn some interesting points about architecture. In addition, if someone is skilled in photography, you might get some good tips on how to take better photos. I learned about "poison rings" from a friend, and it was fun to search the shops and markets to see if I could find one. It might be interesting to explore the different categories of interests that one might have and share these with your potential travel companion. You might learn that you have many interests in common that you would like to incorporate into your adventure. It is important to do some things that may not be your interest because you will enrich your own experience. For example, your friend may want to take a cooking class, and you do not. By taking the cooking class, you will probably find something else that you like such as driving through the Tuscan countryside or participating in a wine tasting.

Daily Habits

Sleeping

Are you an early bird or a night owl? Sleeping habits can make or break a trip. There are many advantages to going to bed early and rising early when traveling. However, it is no fun to roam the early morning streets or to see a beautiful sunrise with a grumpy, sleep-deprived friend. Street noise and snoring can interfere with your usual seven to eight hours of uninterrupted sleep. I travel with a CPAP machine that prevents my snoring from disturbing others. Most people over sixty do snore. When I was twenty-five, I did not even know if people snored!

Exercise

If you are used to exercising every day, it is important to maintain that habit when traveling. Fortunately, travel itself is usually a lot of exercise whether walking for miles around a city or climbing five flights of stairs to see a beautiful palace. Your physical condition will determine how many miles you walk or how many steps you will climb. If you are an early morning jogger, it is important to consider safety. Maybe you could jog around a plaza while your arthritic friends savor a caffe latte in a nearby café. In addition, it is just as important to wait patiently for a friend with arthritis who needs to rest every once in awhile.

Food/Diet

Everyone has a special way of eating. For some it might mean eating a hearty breakfast or eating dinner early. In the Golden Years, many have problems with gallbladders, hiatus hernias, and irregularity. Spicy or greasy food may not be an option for some. Some of us follow a strict diet of healthy eating while some of us just like to eat, period! It is important to make sure no one is going hungry or experiencing low blood sugar by skipping meals just because you want to make it to a museum line early in the morning.

Food is probably the most expensive item in your travel budget. It is beneficial to plan to eat as many meals as possible in your apartment or to take picnic lunches or snacks with you when you are out traveling for the day. However, who can resist a lunch in a beautiful cafe overlooking the cityscape or watching gondolas glide by? One advantage to eating out in a restaurant is that they usually have nice restrooms.

Neatness

When you are staying in an apartment, you do not have room service. I think it is considerate to make your bed, clean up in the bathroom, empty trash, wash dishes, and keep your belongings neat and tidy.

You may think that all of this information about personal characteristics is excessive, but I cannot emphasize enough how important your travel companions are to the enjoyment of your trip.

CHAPTER 2:
Getting Ready

In this chapter, you will learn about all of the things that you need to do before you go on a trip to Italy. By preparing well, you will enjoy your trip much more and avoid many of the stresses that may come from traveling. In our Golden Years, most of us have our "senior moments" where we forget important items or events. This chapter can serve as a checklist so that you will not forget important details.

Passport

It is a good idea to make sure you have a current passport as soon as you start thinking about traveling because it can take anywhere from four to six weeks to obtain a passport. The easiest way to obtain your passport is to go on-line to either www.travel.state.gov or www.usps.com/passport/welcome. htm. They have two kinds of applications: one for renewals and one for first time passports. A passport is valid for ten years. You have to apply for a new passport if your passport is more than fifteen years old. The fee is usually around $100. You can also go to the post office, get an application, and mail it in.

I also recommend registering with the U.S. Consulate when you are going to be out of the country for a month or more. They can contact you if there is an international emergency of some sort, hopefully not terrorism; they also keep you up to date on health issues like the swine flu and immunizations. You can receive a lot of good information on their Web site at http://travelregistration. state.gov.

Money

Italy uses the Euro as their currency. The conversion rate varies weekly. You can get the most current rates at the Web site: www.xe.com/ucc/. The Euro for 2009 has varied from $1.28 per dollar to $1.51 per dollar. If the Euro is $1.45, something that costs around $10.00 here at home will cost $14.50 when using Euros. Do not use cash express centers in Italy because they will charge you exorbitant fees. The best way to get Euros is to use your debit card at Bancomats (ATMs) in Italy. There are Bancomats all over, including at the airport. You can also use credit cards for many purchases in established stores and large restaurants.

Make sure you check with your bank or your credit card company before you go to notify them that you will be traveling outside of the United States. I know several people who did not and found out they could not use their card in Italy. Also, make sure you have the phone numbers to report a lost or stolen card with you. You might also want to check with your bank to find out what their conversion rates are. For example, Wells Fargo banks charge $5 per transaction. Also, check your daily credit limit. I would recommend that you have at least a $500 daily limit so that you do not have to use the Bancomats so often. Most Bancomats limit withdrawals to 250 Euros but some will allow 350 Euros. If the Euro exchanges at $1.30, that will cost you $455.

Register with your bank on-line so that you can check your bank account to keep track of your balance. It is also a good way to keep track of how much you are spending and to deduct conversion expenses. In Italy, they have little Internet cafes every few blocks. You must give them your passport for identification (I guess they have some homeland security rules, too) and pay around one Euro for thirty minutes. You can also read your e-mail and send messages to friends and family.

I also recommend that you have a friend with you to cover your back while you are using the Bancomat. Cover the keypad when you enter your PIN.

Setting Your Travel Dates

A great advantage to being retired is that you can travel whenever you want. When planning your itinerary, consider the weather, location, tourist seasons, and special events. It is important to check with the airlines when you set your travel dates, as some do not have flights to Italy every day. Use your calendar to plan around holidays and weekends. Many of the tourist sites such as churches are closed on Sundays. Many museums are closed on Mondays. The cost of airline tickets varies with the day you fly. Usually, Saturdays, Tuesdays, and Wednesdays are cheaper.

Weather in Italy varies with season and location. You can consult with the Web site, www.weather.com, to find out average temperatures and precipitation by month. Our personal thermostats vary a lot in our Golden Years. Some of us are still having hot flashes while others need a sweater if the temperature dips slightly. Northern Italy is close to the Alps so it is usually cooler there in the summer. However, the winters are more severe than in the southern part of the country. Many of the boat excursions on Lake Como and Lake Maggiore do not run in the winter months. The ferries in Cinque Terra usually stop running in October until March or April. The temperatures in the southern part of Italy are very hot in the summer, but they are usually pleasant in the fall, winter, and spring. Most of Italy is very hot in July and August. If you plan to go to Venice, it is best to avoid late October, November, and December because of the flooding called *acqua alta*. St. Mark's Piazza may be underwater and you will need boots to walk the streets.

Italy is a very popular tourist site in general. Students and children crowd the tourist sites in the summer. Many like to visit during the Christmas season and at Easter. Most Italians take their vacations in August. Because of this, many restaurants and shops close their doors in August. The Italians head to the coastal towns and beaches causing overcrowding in those places.

You will also want to consider special events. For example, if you want to see the *Historica Regata* (gondola parade) in Venice, you will have to plan to be there the first Sunday in September. In Appendix 4, I have listed festivals and harvests that you may want to consider in planning your itinerary. My favorite travel months are May, September, and early October.

Train Passes

Eurail train passes are the best value for train travel. Their value depends on how long you are staying and how many trips you plan to make. A two-month first class pass for ten days costs around $465. A two-month first-class pass for three days costs $249. Their Web site is www.eurail.com. Order your tickets early, as they are delivered by mail to your home address.

On a two-month pass, you can choose three to ten travel days. If you do not have a pass, the train tickets will cost $175–185 roundtrip on the Eurostar from Florence to Rome or Venice. Many of the day trip destinations from Florence use local trains or buses that are less expensive. I have included some of my favorite railway and bus schedules in the chapters for visiting different cities. You can also go to www.RailEurope.com or www.trentitalia.it to check other schedules. Once I know where and when I am going, I check the RailEurope Website to determine what trains I will take. They update the schedules every year in June. For example, if I want to go to Rome for the day from Florence, I choose Eurostar AV 9551 that leaves Florence at 8:40 AM and arrives in Rome at 10:05. If you take an intercity train, it will take you over an hour longer. I leave Rome at 6:45 PM and arrive in Florence at 8:20 PM. Always buy your tickets a day or two ahead of time for first-class seats.

Apartment

When you look for an apartment or hotel, always check to see if they have an elevator (lift). Many of the apartments I checked did not have an elevator, and they often had two or three flights of stairs.

I have found an excellent apartment in Florence that is not expensive when you have at least four people in your group, about $43 a night per month or $47 a night for two weeks. Even though the Website offers prices for daily or weekly rates, you will save a lot by staying for two weeks or more. This site can accommodate up to seven people. If you plan to use this apartment, use the Website, www.residenzarondinelli.it. The phone number is 39 055 6818199; the cell is 39 339 4362363. The Web site has many choices, but I like the Rondinelli 2 called "Fresco." It has two large bedrooms (plus a double hide-a-bed in the living room and a single hide-a-bed in one of the bedrooms), three full marble bathrooms with showers, a modern kitchen, living room, and dining room. The kitchen has a microwave, gas stove and oven, dishwasher, refrigerator, and most needed kitchen utensils, cooking pans, and dishes. This apartment has very good air conditioning and heating. It has a small washing machine, but Italy does not have clothes dryers. This is because they are very conservative in using electrical energy. You have to hang up your wet clothes, but they do have drying racks. This apartment also has very high, beautifully painted ceilings. It is furnished with antique and comfortable furniture. The apartment was completely refurbished in 2008. It is quite large and very clean.

The apartment also has a flat screen TV, DVD player, and Internet connections. There are many Golden Agers nowadays who have laptops. Because it is one more thing to carry, I prefer to stop in the Internet cafes. The TV stations are limited, but we enjoyed BBC and a station that shows funny home videos. You will need adapters for your media equipment, CPAP (if used), and battery chargers. Check all of your equipment to see if it is suitable for 240 current. In the United States, we use 120 current. You may need converters if your equipment is not set for 120/240 currents. You can purchase these in most large department stores, in travel stores, and on the Internet. You should not use your own hair dryer and curling iron because they can still overheat even with converters. The apartment has nice hair dryers in the bathrooms.

The location is the best of all the apartments I have searched. It is located 200 meters, about 200 yards, from the train station and about 300 meters from the Duomo. It is in a very nice area next to the famous fashion avenue, Via Tornabuoni. We walk to the train station in about ten minutes. There are also taxis if you prefer. It is on the first floor which, in Italy, is the second floor. There are about seven steps up to the elevator or lift. It has a small elevator that is great for getting your luggage up to the apartment or for those who do not like steps. You will have to pay around ten per cent down to reserve the apartment, and it is a good idea to plan far in advance to get the dates you want. They will refund the money up to sixty days before your reservation date. When you arrive, you must pay the balance in Euros. There is a Bancomat directly below the apartment. Before you go, they will give you a phone number to call to meet the rental agent at the apartment. They prefer that you arrive before 5 PM.

Door to the Rondinelli 6 Apartment

Living room in the Apartment

They also have a second apartment called "Open Space." It is a studio apartment for two to four people. The beds are located above the living area up a spiral staircase. I do not recommend this apartment if you need to get up in the night to use the bathroom or if you want to avoid extra stairs.

You can also research the hundreds of apartments available in Florence. Location, accessibility, and price are primary considerations. If you Google "apartments in Florence, Italy," you will find several Web sites listing apartments. Their definition of a "few steps" often means several blocks. If you do not find one near the train station, you will be doing a lot of walking with luggage. Of course, taxis are not expensive and they are always lined up right outside the train station.

Trains

Boarding the train, when you are already familiar with the station and the system, takes no more than a few minutes. However, when you are new to a country, things always get more difficult. Even if you have purchased your tickets ahead of time, it is always better to show up at the station at least twenty or thirty minutes before the train's scheduled departure. This will allow you enough time to get familiar with the station, to locate the platform from which the train will depart, and, if needed, to buy some food and drinks to take on the train. Espresso, Interregionale, Regionale, and Diretto trains usually do not have a bar or a cart from which you can buy food and drinks. The EuroStar provides small drinks and snacks for no extra charge. They also have a dining car or snack bar. The restrooms on the trains are usually clean and good-sized. Most of the trips in Italy from Florence are less than three hours.

For the most part, you will be traveling between large cities like Florence, Rome, and Venice. Therefore, obviously, the larger the station, the more time you will need to get oriented. If you have to purchase tickets, add at least fifteen minutes just to be extra sure you will not be late. I usually purchase tickets (*biglietti*) at least a day in advance because the Eurostar requires seat reservations. That way you also know exactly what time the train departs and arrives. You can also buy tickets ahead for the regional trains even though they have no reservations. Most of the personnel in the ticket offices speak English.

In the larger train stations, they post very good schedules. You can check to see if your train is on time and also to locate what platform *(binario)* you need to find. It is not unusual for them to change the platform number so it always good to check the signs continually. In the larger cities, the train platforms will provide signs where the car numbers are located. Sometimes the first car may be at the far end. Check your ticket for the car number (*carrozo*). Always make sure you stamp your ticket in the little yellow boxes on the platforms before you board unless you have reservations. The conductor will come through the train to check your tickets.

The main train station in Florence is the *Santa Maria Novella, S.M.N.* It is a very large train station with a McDonald's restaurant and little shops where you can buy postcards, bus tickets, and snacks. On the lower level of this train station, there is a shopping area with many shops for clothing, shoes, accessories, and cosmetics. The restrooms are on the lower floor and charge around one Euro to use them. Escalators are available during the day. At night, they often turn them off.

Roma Termini is the main station in Rome. It is a very large, busy station. It also has many shops and several restaurants. The main train station in Venice is called *Santa Lucia*. It is located right on the Grand Canal. I use this station for one-day trips. When I stay overnight, I prefer to stay in the town called Mestre, just outside Venice. I use the *Mestre* station that stops before the *Santa Lucia* station. Always make sure you designate which station you want when you purchase your tickets.

Packing

I have prepared a packing list that you will find in Appendix 6. It includes just about everything you may need. I recommend that you try to get by with a carry-on suitcase (with wheels, of course), a travel bag, and your waist pack. Lately, airlines will only allow two carry-on items so you will have to fit your waist pack into your travel bag. If you have back or knee problems, even a piece of luggage with wheels can become very heavy when walking through airports or boarding trains. I use a travel security waist pack that you can find at www.CorporateTravelSafety.com for about $40. It also has zipper locks for the compartments. That is very important to prevent pickpockets. You can order a large waist pack that is roomy enough for your cameras and video camcorder. It is also important to have a neck pouch that you can pin inside your shirt or underwear. In here, I keep my passport, money, and credit cards.

Your packing list will vary according to the season in which you are traveling. The most important thing is to travel light. You can buy almost anything you need once there. On the way home, you can check the bag. I do not like to take chances on lost luggage on my way there. Leave your jewelry at home!

If you plan to do a lot of shopping, I recommend that someone in your group check an empty bag. When you return home, you can pack your purchases and check the bag. Even with the extra fee, it will be much cheaper than sending a large package. You will have to pay custom fees if you have over $800 per person.

Batteries

If original packaging is not available for spare batteries, effectively insulate battery terminals by isolating the batteries from contact with other batteries and metal. Do not permit a loose battery to come in contact with metal objects, such as coins, keys, or jewelry. Place each battery in its own protective case, plastic bag, or package. If the batteries are unpackaged, you should place tape across the contacts to isolate the terminals. Isolating the terminals prevents short-circuiting.

Liquids

The airline policy is 3-1-1 for carry-on: <u>3.4</u> ounces or less for bottles (by volume); <u>1</u> quart-sized, clear, plastic, zip-top bag; <u>1</u> bag per passenger placed in the screening bin. One quart bag per person limits the total liquid volume each traveler can bring. The 3.4 oz. container size is a security measure. If in doubt, put your liquids in checked baggage. Be prepared. Each time security personnel have to hand search a carry-on, it slows down the line. Practicing 3-1-1 will ensure a faster and easier checkpoint experience.

Declare larger liquids, medications, baby formula, food, and breast milk. Some brave Golden Agers like to take their grandchildren or great-grandchildren with them. Airlines allow these liquids in reasonable quantities exceeding three ounces, and they are not required to be in the zip-top bag. Declare these items for inspection at the checkpoint. You may bring all prescription and over-the-counter medications (liquids, gels, and aerosols) including petroleum jelly, eye drops, and saline solution for medical purposes. I put these in a separate zip-top bag.

Additional items you may bring include: liquids necessary for a disability or medical condition; life-support and life-sustaining liquids such as bone marrow, blood products, and transplant organs; items used to augment the body for medical or cosmetic reasons such as mastectomy products, prosthetic breasts, gels inserts, saline solution, or other liquids; and, gels or frozen liquids needed to cool medically related items.

You are not limited in the amount or volume of these items that you bring in your carry-on baggage. However, if the medically necessary items exceed three ounces or are not contained in a one-quart, zip-top plastic bag, you must declare them to one of the security officers at the checkpoint for further inspection. I also bring a note from my doctor explaining why I need these items. Most security agents have become familiar with CPAP machines, but it is also a good idea to have a note from your doctor. Place your CPAP machine in a separate bin, as they will have to run it through a special machine.

Insurance

I recommend that you sign up for travel insurance. In recent years, Italy has experienced earthquakes and volcanoes. I use the Web site for www. insuremytrip.com. I like the American Express Global Travel Shield Classic Package that costs about $102 for a $2000 trip. This price covers your airfare and most pre-paid expenses. It includes $25,000 medical, $2,000 trip cancellation, and $2,000 for baggage. When you travel on your own, most hotels have a 48-hour cancellation policy.

Make sure you have both medical coverage and trip insurance. They will send you a copy of the insurance plan. Take it with you or have it available on your e-mail file. Luckily, I have never had to use it, but one bad fall will make it worthwhile. In addition, it is good for peace of mind. Their phone number is 1-800-487-4722. Outside the United States, the phone number is 1-401-773-9300.

Cell Phones

It is convenient to have a cell phone with you, particularly if you need to keep in touch with someone at home. Our cell phones usually do not work in Italy. If you are traveling with several people, more than one phone is helpful to stay in contact with each other. Order your phones in advance so that you will have your number to give your friends and family at home. They will send you detailed instructions on-line. I have used Cellular Abroad (CA). They have provided good service and reasonable rates. You can reach them by phone, 1-800-287-5072, or by e-mail: orders@cellularabroad.com

All cell phone rentals include: a GSM cellular phone; international plug adapters; international 110-220 volt charger; phone box; a user guide; a return shipping label; and, a SIM card for Italy. To add credit to your account, purchase a recharge card and enter the unique code into the handset. It is available through Cellular Abroad and in Italy. You can call CA and they will read the code over the phone. They also send you a text message with the code. Additional cards are $29 for forty-two minutes of outgoing talk time to the United States, and as much as eighty-five minutes in Italy. You can receive unlimited incoming calls from anywhere. Voicemail is free. If you are using a lot of minutes, make sure you save enough minutes to call in to the company for recharge cards.

For the first time, you will pay a $150 security deposit per phone minus the rental period fee upon the phone's return, $29 for initial talk time (one per phone), and $29 for round trip shipping. The second time I rented one phone; the cost was $105.88 for the rental phone and one phone card. The phone usually comes charged. Just insert the SIM chip into the SIM card slot. When I received my phone, the SIM card was already in the phone. Phones are covered by your credit card insurance because you are actually purchasing the phone, and then, CA is buying it back. Make sure you charge your phone before you leave. Make sure you take the directions with you.

Unless you have to keep in touch with someone back home, you can get by without a cell phone. I like the convenience of calling ahead for the apartment or hotel or to verify services such as limos and hotel shuttles. E-mail is the best way to communicate with those back home. At the Internet cafes located in almost every neighborhood, you will only pay one Euro for thirty minutes. We actually only used our cell phone five times during a month in Italy, but we used the Internet almost every day. Most hotels offer free Internet access.

Although pay phones are becoming rare, there are modern public pay phones in major areas like train stations and airports, and on major streets. If you are calling from a pay phone, you need to insert a phone card or a one Euro coin. It is best to buy a phone card, *carta telefonica*, which usually comes in denominations of three Euros to thirty Euros. Once in Italy, you can purchase a phone card at any newsstand, bar, or *tabaccheria*. Ask for *una scheda telefonica*. For some cards, you must snap off the perforated corner of the card or it will not fit into the slot on the phone.

Phone calls

When calling to Italy, dial 011-39 plus the city code and phone number. When calling in Italy omit 011-39. Italian phone numbers have two parts: area code and phone number. The area code is from two to four digits and begins with a zero, unless it is a cell phone; then, it begins with a three. Example area codes: Rome–06, Florence– 055, Siena–0577, Venice–041. The phone number has six or seven digits. When calling locally, you must use the city code for that city. Dial the city code, even if you are dialing from the same city.

To call to the United States from Italy, dial the United States long distance code–00, the country code–1, and then the area code and number.

To call home collect, you can use your U.S. phone company calling card; just call the phone company's toll-free access number: AT&T 800-172-444. If you have another long-distance carrier, be sure to call them before leaving home to get your access number for Italy.

CHAPTER **3:**
Planning Your Itinerary

It is helpful to plan your itinerary. There are so many places to go in Italy that you have to set some priorities. For example, we knew we wanted to ride a gondola in Venice, see the Sistine Chapel in Rome, and go to Siena, Lucca, and Portofino. I have included a sample itinerary in Appendix 7. When traveling on your own in your Golden Years, you can eliminate a location if you just want to stay home and rest for the day.

Italy is usually described as shaped like a boot. It is bordered on the north by the European countries of Switzerland, Austria, France, and Slovenia. It is bordered on the west by the Tyrrhenian Sea and on the east by the Adriatic Sea. The Apennine Mountains form the backbone of the country, and the Alps border the North. It is about the size of Arizona.

The northern region has many lakes. The southern region includes the large islands of Sicily and Sardinia. The Po is the largest river. It flows from the Alps on the western side to the Adriatic Sea on the eastern side.

The largest cities are Rome, Milan, Naples, Palermo, Genoa, Bologna, Florence, Bari, Catania, and Venice. Only Rome, Milan, and Naples exceed 1,000,000 in population. Italy is divided into twenty regions. If you search for "Italy Heaven" on your computer, you will find lists of popular destinations from large cities to small towns.

You will find detailed information on traveling to Milan, Venice, and Rome in the following chapters. I have also provided more information on the day trips in Chapter 14. It is easy to travel from Florence. It is very convenient to take the bus or train to many towns surrounding Florence and then return to your apartment in the evening. A great advantage is that you do not have to deal with your luggage. I love just walking out of the apartment with my waist pack and a small bag to pack a lunch, snacks, a book, and a map. Unlike a tour, I do not have to get up at the crack of dawn, and I can return home whenever I get tired.

CHAPTER 4:
Getting There

Once you have chosen your travel dates and have carefully selected your travel companions, you will need to make your plane reservations. Most flights from the United States enter Italy through Rome or Milan. I like Delta and United because they have one-stop flights to Italy. For example, you can fly from Albuquerque, New Mexico to Atlanta, Georgia and then continue your flight to Milan or Rome. Those airlines offer the shortest routes and are usually the least expensive. For us Golden Agers, the shortest route means less walking through airports. Sometimes it is cheaper to go directly to the airline, but sometimes you will get the best deal by surfing between travel Websites such as Expedia or Orbitz. Flights can vary from $770 to over $2000. Since this book is based on staying in Florence, I have included how to get from airports to train stations for trains that will take you to Florence.

To Milan:
From the Malpensa airport in Milan, take the Malpensa Shuttle bus to go to the *Milano Centrale* train station. You will need to make sure you take the Malpensa Express that goes to the *Milano Centrale* train station, as there are buses that go to another train station. You buy your tickets in the airport but the bus leaves from the front of the airport. There are Bancomats (ATMs) in the airport. The trip usually takes about forty minutes and costs seven Euros. When you arrive at the train station, you go inside to purchase your tickets and to board the train to Florence.

To Rome:
Take the Leonardo Express for eleven Euros to go to the *Termini* train station.

There you will take the train to Florence. Try to get the Eurostar, as it is faster and nicer.

To Florence:
A shuttle bus takes about twenty minutes to get from the airport to the *Santa Maria Novella* train station. There are not many flights to Florence. The flights that do fly into Florence usually require several changes.

To Venice:
When you arrive at the airport, take the A.T.A.F. bus to the *Mestre* train station for three Euros. There you will take the train to Florence. If you are going to visit Venice, you can take another bus that goes right into Venice. See Chapter 11 for information about visiting Venice.

To Pisa:
There are about five trains a day that connect the *Pisa Centrale* train station to the Florence train station, *Santa Maria Novella, S.M.N.* A short bus ride connects the Pisa airport to the Pisa train station; the bus ride only costs a little over one Euro. You only pay around 5.7 Euros for a train ticket from Pisa to Florence. You will save money by not using your Eurailpass from Milan, Venice, or Rome. Trains from these cities will use one of your ten days or cost around $85–$100 each way. The train ride from Pisa to Florence only takes about forty-five minutes. However, flights to Pisa usually require at least two stops. All in all, going and coming, you will save two days on your Eurailpass by arriving in Pisa.

The train from Milan takes about two and half hours, and the train from Rome takes about one and half hours (if you catch the Eurostar). The main advantage to flying into Milan or Rome is that you can fly with only one intermediary stop. Personally, I like the one-stop flights because of shorter flying time, a lot less walking, and less lifting of your luggage to the overhead bins.

Time

Changes in time zones can be confusing. For a simple way to figure out what time it is at home, subtract the number of hours of difference between home and where you are. For example, if you live in the Pacific Time Zone, you subtract nine hours. If it is 4 PM in Italy, it is 7 AM in Los Angeles. If you live in the Mountain Time Zone, the difference is eight hours; in the Central

Time Zone, the difference is seven hours; in the Eastern Time Zone, the difference is six hours. Italy only has one time zone. There is a useful Web site at www.timeanddate.com that you can use to figure out what time it is at home.

In 1996, the European Union (EU) standardized European Union Summertime, or Daylight Saving Time (DST). The EU's version of Daylight Savings Time runs from the last Sunday in March (when the clocks go forward by an hour) through to the last Sunday in October (when they go back by an hour).

In Italy, time is based on the 24-hour day and not on the 12-hour clock. 1 PM is expressed as 13:00, 2 PM is 14:00 and 6 PM is expressed as 18:00. They do not use AM or PM. The easiest way to figure out the time is to subtract twelve from the times after twelve o'clock noon. For example, if the time in Italy were 15:00, the time on your watch would be 3:00 (15 - 12). It is important to know the 24-hour-day system for train schedules and for the opening and closing times for locations such as museums and restaurants.

To inquire about time, you should learn these expressions:

Scusi, sa che ore sono? Excuse me, do you know the time?
Tutti i giorni: everyday
A volte: sometimes
Due volte al giorno: twice a day
Sono le due e quindici: It is fifteen minutes after two.
Sono le quattro: It is 4:00 (4:00 a.m.)
Sono le seidici: It is 16:00 (4:00 p.m.)

CHAPTER 5:
Getting Settled

Exchange money

The best way to exchange money is by ATM or Bancomat. You should withdraw some Euros from the Bancomat at the airport when you arrive for expenses like buses, food, bathrooms, and the apartment rental. You will have to pay for the apartment in Euros. They do not take credit cards. You might have to arrange with them to withdraw more money the next day depending on your allowable daily withdrawal limit.

You can also convert some money to Euros before you leave home at your bank, but the exchange rate is usually higher. There is a Bancomat right below the apartment. Banks are located every few blocks around the apartment, down Via Cerratini, and in the Piazza Repubblica. Banks are open 8:30–13:30 (8:30 AM–1:30 PM) and 15:00–16:00 (3–4 PM)

Use ATMs that are located in well-lit public areas, or that are secure inside a bank or a business. Cover the keypad with one hand as you enter your PIN. Look for gaps, tampered appearance, or other irregularities between the metal faceplate of the ATM and the card reader. Avoid card readers that are not flush with the face of the ATM.

Mailing, shipping

If you buy something that costs over 155 Euros at one location, you can claim a refund on taxes. The item must be purchased in retail shops that display a tax-free sign. Fill out a form at the point of purchase. You will need to have it stamped and checked by Italian customs when you leave the country. You will have to show the receipt and the purchase. At major airports, you can get an immediate refund at specially marked booths. You can also return the form to the vendor who will make the refund by either check or credit card.

In Florence, the main post office is at Via Pelliceria, 3r in the arcade west of Piazza Repubblica. When you are ready to mail items back home, you can go to the post office. It is complicated and they say the mail is unreliable. At the post office, you can mail a two-kilogram box (about five pounds) for nineteen Euros. You will have to send in a copy of your passport and customs form when you receive the package. In addition, the Italian mail system will take 8–10 days to deliver your package.

I choose to use Mailboxes, Etc. on Via della Scala 13r, a few blocks from the Santa Maria Novella Piazza. It costs 133.00 Euro for a large box: 10.5 Kilograms. You can share a large box to reduce the cost. On the customs form the mailer sends out, write "personal items." Have nothing wrapped in paper and no price tags. You will have to fill out a form listing the contents of the box. The box will be mailed directly to your home or designated address.

You can mail postcards in the red mailboxes on the streets and by the entrance to the train station. You can purchase stamps at the *tabaccheria* located in the train station and on most main thoroughfares. Make sure you ask for postcard stamps (*francobello di cartolina*) if you are mailing postcards. A postcard stamp will cost .84 Euros or about $1.05 depending on the exchange rate.

The following list will help you at the post office:

Air mail	*Via Aerea*
Books	*Libri*
Box	*Scatola*
Bubble Wrap	*Pluribol*
Envelope	*Busta*
Cartolina	*Postcard*
Stamp	*Francobollo*
String	*Corda*

Package	*Pacco*
Letter	*Lettura*
Packing tape	*Scotch da Pacci*
Post office	*Uffcio postale*

Unpacking

The bedrooms in Italy do not have closets. They have *armagios* that are like armoires in our country with hanging and drawer space. They also provide hangers so you do not have to bring your own or purchase them.

When staying in an apartment, you do not have to repack or tote your luggage around whenever you go on a short trip. This may not be important to the younger generation, but it is very important to those of us in the Golden Years.

Preparing Meals

One of the great things about staying in an apartment is that you can cook your meals to save money. Even if you do not want to cook, you can at least have breakfast and pack a lunch. I have included some great recipes in Appendix 5.

If you have an apartment, you will want to be familiar with the grocery stores or *negozio di alimentary*. The very large Mercato Centrale, near the San Lorenzo open-air markets, on Via dell'Ariento, is open from 7:00–14:00 (7AM–2 PM) every day except Sunday. It is only open on Saturdays in the winter. It is about a ten-minute walk from the apartment.

From the apartment, go back to the main street, Via Panzani, and go left towards the train station. Go to the first street, Via del Giglio and make a right. Go down about three blocks until you pass the San Lorenzo Church. Turn left on Via dell'Ariento and you will see the big two-story market building. Even if you do not want to buy anything, it is worth the time to see the many shops and displays. The first floor has fish, meats, cheeses, and main course fixings. On the second floor, you will find fruits and vegetables. The market building also has a fresh pasta shop where you can watch them making pasta. Their homemade spinach and ricotta ravioli are wonderful.

For bread, try the *Pany Da Lory Di Maestri Lorena* inside the *Mercato di San Lorenzo*. They have great salted bread, unlike the typical Tuscan unsalted bread. They have all kinds of bread and baguettes. They also sell fresh pasta, cookies, breadsticks, and some cheeses. They sell boxed meals that you can take home and cook yourself. If you tell the clerk that you read about her on Divina Cucina (a TV cooking show), she may give you a discount. For lunch, try *Da Nerbone*. Order a *bollito* (roll) with boiled beef and ask for the au jus sauce. *Molte delicioso!*

Supermercato Conad is a small grocery store where you can pick up typical grocery items like milk, yogurt, condiments, butter, and toilet paper. It is located close to the Rondinelli apartment. Just walk towards the train station on Via Panzani to the Plaza Unita and turn right. The address is Via dei Servi, 56r.

There are few food supermarkets in the city center; these are mainly located in the immediate suburbs. Your rental agent can probably tell you how to get to the other supermarkets. You will have to take a bus.

If you do not feel like cooking, you can go down to Franco's Express, a little deli about two blocks down the main street toward the train station. Franco always has some great Italian dishes, vegetables (I love his cauliflower casserole), pizza, and usually fresh watermelon. He also has a little eat-in area.

Franco's Express Deli

Preparing for emergencies

It is always a good idea to be prepared for emergencies. Walking on uneven sidewalks and on cobblestones creates hazardous situation. One day I did step into a hole and went flying. I landed on my backside and banged my head into a wall. That happened when I was very conscientious about being careful. Fortunately, I had no serious injuries. I actually enjoyed being helped back up by a very kind and handsome Italian man!

Keep these numbers in your purse.

Emergency Phone Numbers
113–Police
112–Carabinieri
118–Ambulance

Emergency Rooms-Hospitals

Policlinico di Careggi
Viale Pieraccini 17 Ph: +39 0554277111
The guidebooks recommend this site for its size and clinical services.

Ospedale di Santa Maria Nuova
Piazza Santa Maria Nuova 1 Ph: +39 05527581
Travel Safety
Tourist Medical Center
Via Lorenzo Magnifico 59
055 475 411 (cash payment only)

For minor health problems, you can try the farmacias; they give more drugs more freely without a prescription than in the United States. Once I had a very bad cold. The pharmacist (*farmacista*) gave me some pills and it was gone the next day! The U.S. Consulate can refer you to an English-speaking doctor if needed.

Pickpockets

Golden Agers should exercise caution at train stations, airports, nightclubs, bars, and outdoor cafes, particularly at night. Criminals are looking for potential victims in such settings. Individuals under the effect of alcohol may become victims of crime, including robbery and assault, due to their impaired ability to judge situations and make decisions. This is particularly a problem for younger Americans visiting Italy where the age limit on the sale of alcoholic beverages is lower than in the United States. Be careful because even older people can have one glass of wine too many. When you are a victim of a crime, file a police report and contact the U.S. Consulate. Most cities provide in-country organizations that provide counseling, medical, and legal assistance to certain crime victims.

Petty crimes such as pick pocketing, theft from parked cars, and purse snatching are serious problems, especially in large cities. Pickpockets sometimes dress like businessmen. Tourists should not be lulled into a false sense of security by believing that well-dressed individuals are not potential pickpockets or thieves. Most reported thefts occur at crowded tourist sites, on public buses or trains, or at the major railway stations. Thieves also target clients of Internet cafes in major cities. Tourists who have tried to resist petty thieves on motor scooters have suffered broken arms and collarbones. Always carry shoulder bags toward the inside away from the street.

Thieves in Italy often work in groups or pairs. Pairs of accomplices or groups of children are known to divert tourists' attention so that another can pickpocket them. In one particular routine, one thief throws trash, waste, or ketchup at the victim; a second thief assists the victim in cleaning up the mess; and, the third thief discreetly takes the victim's belongings. Criminals on crowded public transportation slit the bottoms of purses or bags with a razor blade or a sharp knife removing the contents. If you have a travel security bag or waist pack, you can avoid most of these problems. The travel security bag is steel reinforced to prevent slicing. If you decide to rent a car, always lock the car and remove items such as laptops, luggage, cameras, briefcases, and even cigarettes when parked.

The police are usually powerless. Normal clothes cops patrol the streets. They spot the pickpockets and sometimes manage to stop them as they commit the crime. However, the legal system in Italy does not work very well and the pickpockets are usually out again in a couple of days. The best protection is to be prepared. Carry your security waist pack as mentioned in Chapter 2. I recommend that you use a neck pouch that you can pin inside your shirt or underwear. In here, I keep my passport, money, and credit cards.

One rainy evening, I had an experience where someone in front of me kept pushing back into us with an umbrella. I noticed a tug on my waist pack and looked back to see a large man trying to unzip by bag. He "got fooled" because I had locks on my zippers. I yelled *polizia* and he ran away, after I hit him with my umbrella! Yell these words in Italian: *Andare via*, *Uscire da qui*, and *Partirmi sole*.

Generally, I must add, Italy seemed to be safe. We were observant and aware. We always traveled together. When you travel first class on the trains, using your Eurailpass, the conductors provide supervision. The passengers often provide help if needed. When traveling in a group, one person can be on guard if the others wish to take a nap. Your travel companions can also watch your luggage when you go to the restroom.

CHAPTER 6:
Florence

History

The Arno River runs through the city of Florence. This river helped to make Florence an economic center in the early centuries. Florence is the capital of the province of Tuscany. Between the fourteenth and eighteenth centuries, the Medici family ruled Florence. The Medici family gained their power and fortune from banking. The history of the Medici family is an interesting story but difficult to follow as they often repeat names such as Cosimo, Lorenzo, Guiliano, and Ferdinando from generation to generation.

Through banking and commerce, the family acquired great wealth and political influence in the fourteenth century. The family's wealth and political influence increased until Salvestro de' Medici became the de facto dictator of the city. His brutality led to his downfall when he was banished in 1382. The family's fortune then fell until Giovanni di Bicci de'Medici restored their financial fortune. He made the Medici family the wealthiest in Italy.

Giovanni's son, Cosimo il Vecchio (1389–1464), became the real founder of the political power of the family. In a political struggle with another powerful family, the Albizzi, Cosimo lost and was banished, but, because of the support of the people, he was soon recalled in 1434. Although he himself occupied no office, Cosimo il Vecchio ruled the city as uncrowned king for the rest of his life. Under his rule, Florence prospered.

The most famous Medici was Lorenzo, called the Magnificent. He was the grandson of Cosimo il Vecchio. Under his rule from 1469 to 1492, Florence reached its golden age. His brother, Guiliano, shared the power. Conspirators killed Guiliano in 1478 in what historians call the Pazzi scheme. Both a patron of the arts and a tyrant, Lorenzo the Magnificent created a city of magnificent art.

Florence is most famous for its role in the Italian Renaissance. Several historical figures were either born in Florence or chose it as their home: Alighieri Dante, Leonardo da Vinci, Michelangelo, and Galileo Galilei.

Florence took part in the struggle for the independence and re-unification of Italy in the nineteenth century. It was the capital of the kingdom of Italy from 1865 to 1870. In World War I, Italy at first joined Germany and Austria, but it later joined the Allies of England, France, and the United States. During World War II, bombs damaged Florence, but most of the city's treasures survived. In 1966, a devastating flood of the Arno River damaged many works of art. Today, long after its period of greatness, millions of people visit Florence each year to experience its unique art that reflects the greatness of the human spirit.

About Florence

Florence is my favorite city. It is easily accessible from all parts of Italy by train and is located centrally in the country. You can travel between southern Italy and Florence or between northern Italy and Florence in just a few hours by train. There are many cities within an hour's distance from Florence when traveling by bus or train. Many people like to drive, but I prefer to use their excellent transportation system. There are no worries about parking or finding a parking place and especially no worries about accidents or breakdowns. I do not recommend using a car to travel around Florence. They have a very efficient bus system, the A.T.A.F. It goes to every neighborhood and the outlying areas of the city. Even though many areas of Florence are within walking distance, the bus can provide needed relief when your legs start aching or your hip is throbbing. Tickets are available at the *tabaccherias* (tobacco shops) located all over town.

There is a lot of information about Florence on the Internet. I will try to synthesize all that is available to give you an easy plan to see most of Florence. Many guidebooks say that you can easily cover the historical center of Florence by walking. When you have arthritis, walking through a whole city is never easy. However, as you travel at your own pace, you can sit down and rest whenever you want. Actually, strolling is a better term than walking. It is best to see Florence on foot as much as possible, as there are so many interesting buildings and shops on every street. The city itself is so small that you can reach most destinations on a 20-30 minute stroll. Wear comfortable walking shoes. The streets are cobblestones and the sidewalks are narrow.

The multitude of colossal buildings impressed me on my first visit. The Florentines built most of these building in the fourteenth and fifteenth centuries. They are huge with immense arched doorways, heavy wooden doors, and large windows with wooden shutters. There are no screens on the windows. I was amazed at the lack of insects. I saw no moths, flies, ants, or butterflies and, especially, no creepy, crawly things. Because there are few trees or plants within the ancient part of the city, I also saw few birds except for pigeons. I saw no stray dogs and only a few cats. Mosquitoes can be problems in the summer, so keep your windows closed at night. The city keeps the city clean. You will see little street cleaning trucks all over. One morning, before dawn, I saw women sweeping the streets with big straw brooms.

The street numbers in Florence are red for businesses and blue for residences. The red and blue numbers are not consecutive to each other so you can easily get confused if you do not realize there is a different numbering system for red and blue.

Maps

It is important to have a good map of each city that you visit. Airports and train stations all sell maps. I like the fold out pocket maps. I found the best free map of Florence at Mailboxes, Etc. You can also use the Internet to find interactive satellite maps where you can actually "walk" through the streets.

There is an information office right outside the train station and a tourist information office at Via Cavour, 1r. It is open 8:15 AM– 7:15 PM daily and from 8:30 AM–1:30 PM on Saturday. They have information about the city, events, maps, and tourist sites. Ask for the concierge book, a large map of Florence, and a bus route map.

Buses

You can pick up a free A.T.A.F. bus schedule at the bus station just outside the train station. The A.T.A.F. information and ticket office is open daily from 7 AM–7 PM. Bus maps are free.

The A.T.A.F. buses go all over Florence and its surrounding areas. One ride is 1.2 Euro or you can also buy a three-day or weekly pass. A pack of four one-hour tickets costs 4.5 Euro. A 70-minute ticket costs two Euros when you buy it on board, but it costs only 1.20 Euros if you buy it before boarding the bus. A 24-hour ticket costs five Euros. A 3-day ticket costs twelve Euros, and a weekly pass costs twenty-two Euros. The *Carta Agile* is the new A.T.A.F. Smart Card. It holds a chip that has a series of 60-minute tickets. It costs 10 or 20 Euros and is handy for groups of people.

You buy the tickets at the little tobacco shops (*tabaccheria*) all around town. You can buy an A or B ticket and ride the bus all around Florence. For an inexpensive city tour, take bus number 12 or 13. Each makes an hour-long circuit around the city. It is a good way to become familiar with the city. You can also take the orange electric buses (routes A, B, C or D) that are able to navigate Florence's narrow streets.

A large orange sign, Fermata, displays the numbers of the buses that stop at that sign. Orange A.T.A.F. buses circle around the city daily from 6 AM–1 AM. A.T.A.F. maintains over fifty bus lines in Florence. Be sure to use one of the on-bus orange machines to validate your ticket once you are on board the bus. Penalties for riding without a validated ticket are stiff. If the bus is crowded, it is sometimes difficult to get up to the validation machine, but it is important that you have the card stamped.

The S.I.T.A. buses go to the towns surrounding Florence such as Siena and San Gimignano. They are more convenient than the trains for some of the day trips because they usually stop near the center of town. The S.I.T.A. bus station is close to the *Santa Maria Novella* train station. If you leave the station from the south exit, it is just across the street. You purchase your tickets inside. From here, you make connections to most of the smaller towns. You do not need to take a traditional tour bus to get to Siena, San Gimignano, or other neighboring cities. It is so easy and affordable to take the public bus. The buses are nice and comfortable, and they run on a regular schedule. Make sure you get on the bus that does not stop at every little village. The Rapida bus usually skips the little towns.

Taxis

Florentines generally do not use taxis but they are quite convenient for those of us having problems with walking or breathing. You will find many hotels and restaurants along pedestrian-only streets or in little squares that are difficult or impossible to reach by taxi. However, you can find taxis throughout Florence in areas where allowed, like main thoroughfares. If you are traveling with loads of luggage (something I always discourage), taxis are helpful.

Taxi stands are in and near major squares and the train station. You may also call a taxi from a restaurant or hotel (055 42 42 or 055 43 90). Taxis charge .85 Euros per kilometer, with a minimum fare of 2.64 Euros. Between 10 PM and 6 AM, the minimum price jumps to 5.70 Euros. On Sundays and holidays, the minimum price is 4.48 Euros, with an additional, though minimal, extra charge for initial pick-up within the central city. Taxis charge .62 Euros per piece of luggage, and there is a four-bag limit. A customary tip for a taxi journey is 1-2 Euros.

CHAPTER 7:
Tour Florence by Neighborhoods

The best way to tour Florence is by neighborhood. I am always impressed by the antiquity and the abundance of spectacular art in Florence. Most of the buildings are six to seven hundred years old.

The following neighborhoods are all located in the historical part of Florence. You can visit an interactive map of Florence at www.italyguides.it to find the main streets in this area. I will list a landmark starting point in each neighborhood and give directions to the sites in that neighborhood.

As I describe each neighborhood, you may find more information than you need. As I have said before, in the Golden Years, you may not want to see everything. There are many piazzas where you can rest. I always like to stop in a café for an espresso or *gelato* (ice cream). Always remember that travel is not a job and that it should be fun.

The Neighborhood of Santa Maria Novella

This neighborhood begins at the Santa Maria Novella train station. Take Via degli Avelli to Piazza Santa Maria Novella. Santa Maria Novella is a large church at the end of the piazza. Across the street from the train station, the area around Piazza Santa Maria Novella is perhaps the most varied neighborhood in the city. The dingier, urban streets leading to the station get a lot of traffic (both automobile and human) while the other side of the grassy Piazza is formed by narrow, serpentine little streets, interesting buildings, and top-notch shopping. The piazza is usually crowded with tourists and the pickpockets preying on them. The train station, the Arno River, and the shopping street, Via Tornabuoni, provide the borders of this neighborhood.

To visit the church you must buy a ticket. The church is very important in the history of Florence. It is full of art masterpieces including Masaccio's *Trinity*.

Basilica of Santa Maria Novella

The church, the adjoining cloister, and the chapterhouse contain a store of art treasures and funerary monuments. In the next chapel, you will see the Brunelleschi wooden crucifix. The major chapel (Tornabuoni) is in the center. The frescoes are by Ghirlandaio. The most important Florentine families financed the project ensuring themselves of funerary chapels on consecrated ground.

This church is called *Novella* (New) because it was built on the site of the ninth century church of Santa Maria delle Vigne. When the site was assigned to the Dominican Order in 1221, they decided to build a new church and an adjoining cloister. Fra Sisto Fiorentino and Fra Ristoro da Campi, Dominican friars, designed the church. Building began in the mid-thirteenth century (about 1246). It was not finished until 1360. On a commission from Giovanni di Paolo Rucellai, a local textile merchant, Leone Battisti Alberti designed the upper part of the inlaid black and white marble facade of the church (1456–1470). The facade of Santa Maria Novella was completed by Leon Battista Alberti in 1470.

Santa Maria Novella was the first great basilica in Florence, and it is the city's principal Dominican church. The vast interior is based on a basilica plan, designed as a Latin cross. It is divided into a nave, two aisles with stained-glass windows, and a short transept. *The Holy Trinity*, situated almost halfway in the left aisle, is an early Renaissance work of Masaccio, showing his new ideas about perspective and mathematical proportions. Look at it carefully and think that, when he died, Masaccio was only twenty-seven years old! Masaccio is as well-known for his contribution to the art of painting as Brunelleschi is for architecture and Donatello is for sculpture. The patrons are the kneeling figures of the judge and his wife, members of the Lenzi family. The cadaver tomb below carries the epigram: "I was once what you are, and what I am you will become." In the sixteenth century, Giambologona created the bronze crucifix on the main altar. The choir (or the *Cappella Tornabuoni*) contains another series of famous frescoes, by Dominico Ghirlandaio and his apprentice, the young Michelangelo (1485–1490). Filippo Brunelleschi designed the pulpit, commissioned by the Rucellai family in 1443. This pulpit has a particular historical significance, because it is where Galileo suffered the first attack on his life. Galileo was persecuted because of his scientific revelations that were disputed by the Catholic church.

The Spanish Chapel (*Cappellone degli Spagnoli*) is the former chapterhouse of the monastery. It is situated at the north side of the green Cloister (*Chiostro Verde*). Buonamico (Mico) Guidalotti commissioned it as his funerary chapel. Construction started around 1343, and it was finished in 1355. The Guidalotti chapel was later called Spanish Chapel because Cosimo I assigned it to Eleonora of Toledo and her Spanish retinue. The Spanish Chapel contains a smaller Chapel of the Most Holy Sacrament.

Piazza Santa Maria Novella.

Here we are again, outside in the square (*piazza*). The square in front the church was used by Cosimo I for the yearly chariot race (*Palio dei Cocchi*). This custom existed in 1563 until late in the nineteenth century. The two obelisks marked the start and the finish of the race. They were set up to imitate an antique Roman circus. The obelisks rest on bronze tortoises, made in 1608 by the sculptor Giambologna. Recently, they have renovated the piazza with new stone paving and comfortable benches where you can just sit and enjoy the ambience of people coming and going.

In front of the facade, you can see an arcade on the right where you turn right onto Via della Scala. On the right, you can enter into one of the most ancient European pharmacies, Santa Maria Novella Pharmacy. This is where the friars prepared and sold medicines. It is a good place to buy any kind of medication, perfumes, herbs, and lotions. They are famous for their potpourri and face creams. Further down the street is an Internet cafe. Across the street, on Via della Scala, you will find a nice shop, Pelletteroa Gioia Chiara, where you can buy leather handbags, wallets, and purses. It is a locally owned shop where they make their own products right in the shop. Mailboxes, Etc. is located next door.

Now return to the Piazza Santa Maria Novella on Via della Scala. The streets in this area are narrow and can be confusing. Via della Scala will turn into Via del Sole. Go about two blocks beyond the piazza to Via del Moro. Turn left on Via del Moro and then go right onto Via del Trebbio. This will end at Via Tornabuoni. It is Florence's finest shopping street. During your walk from here to the river, you can admire Palazzo Strozzi, Palazzo Rucellai, and the church of Santa Trinita.

Palazzo Strozzi

You will recognize the Palazzo Strozzi by the huge stones covering the facade. Filippo Strozzi had the Palace built in 1489. He was considered "the richest man in the world" and was a friend of Lorenzo the Magnificent. This is a masterpiece of fifteenth century Florentine architecture. Strozzi died in 1491, just two years after the builder laid the first stone. It was twenty-five years later, in 1504, when the Strozzi family finally moved into the palace. In 1913, the descendents of the Strozzi family bequeathed the palace to the State. This bequest included the sculptures by Ghirlandaio, Fillippino Lippi, and Orcagna.

The art exhibitions of contemporary art are open 9 AM– 1 PM and 2 PM–6 PM Monday through Friday. Admission is 20 Euros but the ticket is good for a whole year.

The Palazzo Strozzi is much more than great exhibitions. The imposing doors of the Palazzo are open from 9 AM– 8 PM year-round even when there is not an exhibition open. In addition to its new Centre for Contemporary Culture Strozzina (CCCS), the palace also has a new café, a permanent exhibition on the history of the Palazzo Strozzi, wireless Internet, courtyard seating, and a program of concerts, lectures, and events. If you want to splurge, go into the Osteria Tornabuoni on the ground floor of the Strozzi Palazzo and try the meringata, two crispy meringue discs filled with frozen whipped cream and shards of chocolate topped with a warm chocolate and espresso sauce.

The Palazzo Strozzi is family friendly. The palace provides a wide variety of activities for the whole family including special interactive activities for children and special booklets in Italian and in English.

Via Tornabuoni

It is fun to look into the designer shops along Via Tornabuoni. The shopkeepers display the prices in the windows. This probably keeps most people from going inside. Here you will see Gucci, Versace, Valentino, and Armani. Along the street paved in cobblestones, it is fun to window shop and to sample a pastry at Giacosa, Via Tornabuoni, 83r. Also, try the truffles at the shop called Procacci, at Via Tornabuoni, 64r. The *panini tartufati* are tiny sandwiches with truffle pate. They also sell regional hams and other goodies.

Cenacolo del Ghirlandaio, (in Convento di Ognissanti)

From Via Tornabuoni, near the Palazzo Strozzi, to the right, take Via della Spada. Turn left onto Via del Moro. Near the end of this street toward the river you will find Osteria di Giovanni on your right, a wonderful restaurant. I first visited this restaurant in 1972 and it continues to be my favorite. I usually have the *pappa del pomodoro* (tomato bread soup), and the *bistecca di Florentina* (Porterhouse steak). The atmosphere is elegant and the patrons are mostly Florentine. The owner of this restaurant is a gracious host who will seat you and make you feel very welcome.

Continue walking down via del Moro toward the river. When you enter the little piazza, turn to the right to Borgo Ognissanti. On your left across the street at Via Borgo Ognissanti, 11r, you will find a great Lastrucci Italian ceramics store. If you are looking for beautiful Italian ceramics, the La Botega d'Arte is an excellent choice. I could not resist buying beautiful jars, gold embossed trays, and olive oil bottles. It has been in the Lastrucci family for centuries. They will also ship your purchases free of charge and help you avoid customs. One of their best customers is William Shatner, Captain Kirk of Star Trek.

Try the Caffe San Carlo di Lillo on Borgo Ognissanti, 32-34 r. for your morning coffee or breakfast. They have wonderful omelets.

As you continue on Borgo Ognissanti, on your right as you enter another piazza, you will find the beautiful church, Church of Ognissanti. The church was first built in 1251 as part of the convent complex founded by the Umiliati, who had come to Florence from Lombardy in 1239. Although Pope Honorius III approved their Order, their fanatical ideal of poverty was considered heretical. It had been founded as a lay congregation for both men and women devoted to Evangelical perfection and poverty, and to physical labor rather than begging. They produced woolen fabrics and glass. The church was remodeled in the fifteenth centuries in the Baroque style.

In the fifteenth century, it became the parish church of wealthy merchants. Amerigo Vespucci, Domenico Ghirlandaio, and Sondro Botticelli were members. Botticelli was buried in this church.

La Cenacola (The Last Supper) frescoed by Domenico Ghirlandaio (1449–1494) is in the refectory of the Convent of Ognissanti. It is very similar to that (by the same painter) in the Convent in San Marco. In Ognissanti, the colors are more vivacious, but the Latin writings and the cat, symbol of betrayal, are missing. The frescoed vaults are not flying vaults but cross vaults. The trees in the background are richer in color than the other painting. The flight of the predatory birds symbolizes the fatal course of events and the peacock symbolizes the Resurrection. The Apostles look to their Master, indicating their need for His instruction and their preoccupation for His fatal destiny. It is not as famous as The Last Supper by Leonardo da Vinci in Milan but just as beautiful. It is only open Wednesday, Thursday, and Friday 9AM–12 PM. The entrance is free.

The Neighborhood of the Duomo

Travel down the main street Via dei Cerratini to the main attraction in Florence, the Duomo of San Giovanni (John the Baptist). You cannot miss Brunelleschi's magnificent dome crowning the rosy marble Cathedral. It is the central meeting point and tourist hub of the city. The streets surrounding the Duomo cater to visitors, with many restaurants (for a price), and exclusive shopping. The Borgo Albizi, which starts behind the Duomo, is more of a boutique street, featuring handmade, original designs in clothing and accessories. Here, you will find many souvenir shops as well as street performers, caricature artists, tourist traps, and pick pockets. This area has recently become a pedestrian-only area.

Battistero di San Giovanni

Piazza del Duomo is a great place to start a walking tour that will uncover some of Florence's historical beauty. Not only is the piazza rich in history, but it is an architectural delight too. One of the first sights you will see is the Battistero di San Giovanni. One of the oldest buildings in the city, the early Florentines dedicated the Battistero to St. John the Baptist. They constructed it in the eleventh century. Besides the beautiful interior, richly decorated with mosaics, you will find the glorious medieval and Renaissance bronze doors by Andrea Pisano and Lorenzo Ghiberti. The doors designed by Ghiberti that the public sees on the Baptistery are replicas. The originals are located nearby at the Museo dell'Opera del Duomo.

Museo dell'Opera del Duomo

You will find this wonderful museum on the piazza of the Duomo, right across from the apse of the cathedral. The apse is at the end opposite to the front doors. Amongst other things, it contains precious sculptures as well as exhibits connected to the buildings that are dotted around the piazza. You will see many of the objects removed for preservation from the Cathedral, Baptistry and Bell Tower. Redone in 1999, it is a very nice museum. It is open daily 9 AM–7:30 PM. Admittance is six Euros.

Cathedral of Santa Maria del Fiore (Duomo)

Cathedral of Santa Maria del Fiore (The Duomo)

In front of the Baptistery is the Cathedral of Santa Maria del Fiore built by Arnolfo di Cambio in 1296 to replace the old Santa Reparata Cathedral. The archaeological remains of this cathedral are in the basement of the present church. They completed the cathedral 150 years later with the addition of the enormous cupola (dome) that sits above the church's transept. Filippo Brunelleschi, a truly gifted Renaissance architect, designed the dome. It is possible to reach the top of the cupola (access is on the right hand side of the church), which is 107 meters from ground level but there is no lift so you will have to climb over 450 steps. I know some people in their Golden Years who can climb the steps. Even though I cannot climb 450 steps, I still appreciate the mastery of Brunelleschi, as the cupola is also extraordinary from the ground up.

The interior of the cathedral itself is also well worth visiting, Even though at times there can be a long line, the interior of the cathedral is amazing. The best time to go is at 8 AM so that you can get in front of the line. Amongst other things, you will be able to see the frescoes beneath the cupola, painted in the second half of the sixteenth century by Vasari and Zucchari. The frescoes cover an area of around 3600 square meters and represent the Last Judgment. It is also interesting to see the Sacristy in the cathedral where, in 1478, Lorenzo de'Medici sought refuge during the Pazzi conspiracy when the conspirators killed his brother Giuliano. Here you will also see the lined marquetries created by a group of artists including Giuliano and Benedetto da Maiano. By the door, there are two frescoes by Paolo Uccello and Andrea del Castagno. When I walk in and see the beautiful frescoes painted on the ceiling of the Duomo, I am breathless. How did they ever get up there to paint such detail?

If you plan to take a tour, enter the sanctuary via the left-side doors. The church is open Monday, Tuesday, Wednesday, and on Fridays from 10 AM–5 PM. On Thursday, it is open from 10 AM–3:30 PM. On Saturday, it opens at 10 AM and closes at 4:45 PM. On Sunday, the sanctuary is open from 1:30 PM–4:45 PM. On the first Saturday of each month, the church is only open from 10 AM–3:30 PM. For information on special holiday hours and more, visit the Duomo's official tourism site.

Campanile di Giotto

As you leave the cathedral, you will see the bell tower, Campanile di Giotto. Giotto, the renowned medieval artist, began work on the tower before his death in the fourteenth century. You can climb to the top if you like to climb hundreds of stairs. I have a better alternative! Just one street over on the corner of Via del Campanile and Via della Ochre, 24r you will find Grom's for gelato.

The Neighborhood of San Lorenzo

Museo delle Capelle Medici

You can enter the San Lorenzo neighborhood from the train station area on Via Sant' Antonino or Via del Giglio. First, you will see the Museo delle Cappelle Medicee, a red brick building with a dome. Started in 1605, these shrines were under construction for centuries. One of the Medici cardinals, Guilio de'Medici, gave Michelangelo the task to design and build the New Sacristy. Guilio de'Medici is remembered in history as Pope Clement VII. The bodies of several Medici family members are interred in the Cappelle Medicee, most notably Lorenzo the Magnificent, Giuliano de' Medici (his brother, killed during the Pazzi Conspiracy of 1478) and all of the Grand Dukes of Tuscany. Typical of a spiritual leader, Giuliano de' Medici was obsessed with the hereafter and the creation of these intricate chapels testifies to that. Because Michelangelo left before he finished the tombs of Guiliano and Lorenzo Medici, they buried them next to the wall. Those interested in drawing will enjoy actual charcoal sketches by Michelangelo's own hand. Admission is four Euros.

Church of San Lorenzo

Next, around the corner to your right, you will see the Church of San Lorenzo (Chiesa di San Lorenzo) also with a dome. It is one of Florence's ancient churches, rebuilt by Filippo Brunelleschi and his architectural team. One of the true Medici churches, it contains the tombs of many of their famous family members, from Giovanni di Averardo and his wife, Piccarda Bueri, to Cosimo il Vecchio, whose tomb is found in the crypt, directly beneath the church's high altar.

San Lorenzo Markets

The San Lorenzo open-air markets are adjacent to the church. San Lorenzo is home to many of the city's foreign population that runs most of the stands at the bustling local market. The area is the cheapest place to shop and snack in the center of the city. Shop through the stands wisely for real leather bags and accessories, and be on the look out for fakes. Italy has now passed a law prohibiting the purchase of fake designer goods. There is a heavy fine involved. The streets around the market are home to kebab stands and Asian markets, as well as cheap clothing and shoe shops. The Mercato Centrale, at Via dell'Ariento, is a large two-story building, near the San Lorenzo markets. See more information about the market in Chapter 3. If you walk about two blocks past the Mercato Centrale on Via dell'Ariento you will run into Via Nazionale. Make a right, go about three blocks more, pass Via Guelfa, and find Oviesse, one of the few department stores in Florence.

While you are in this neighborhood plan to lunch at Fiaschetteria-Trattoria Mario's, Via Rosina, 2r. From the north side of the San Lorenzo Church, take Borga la Noce to Piazza del Mercato Centrale. Florentines flock to this narrow family-run trattoria near San Lorenzo to feast on Tuscan favorites served at simple tables under a wooden ceiling dating from 1536. Look for the green and white striped awning. It is like a cafeteria and you will be seated wherever there is room, which often means with strangers. A favorite dish is *riso al ragù* (rice with ground beef and tomatoes). Their Florentine steak will melt in your mouth. They do not take credit cards. They are closed Sunday and in August. They do not serve dinner and close at 2 PM. Next-door is Pepo, another good place to eat.

Palazzo Medici-Riccardi

Now go back toward the San Lorenzo Basilica. Across from the basilica, you will see Via de'Gori. Take it to Via Cavour and turn left. Here is the Palazzo Medici-Riccardi. This was the early residence of the Medici family. Cosimo the Elder (il Vecchio) commissioned the famed architect, Michelozzo, to build the palace in 1444. From the interior courtyard, you will see the Chapel of the Magi (*Cappella dei Magi*). Piero, the son of Cosimo il Vecchio, ordered the construction of the private chapel. Benozzo Gozzoli created the beautiful frescoes. Throughout the frescoes, he painted portraits of major Florentine figures and members of the Medici family. The state restored the chapel in 1992 for the 500-year anniversary of the death of Lorenzo the Magnificent.

The Medici family lived there until 1537 when a descendant of the brother of Cosimo il Vecchio, Cosimo I, moved the seat of the republic to the Palazzo Vecchio. He became the Grand Duke of Tuscany in 1569. Later the family moved to the larger, grandiose Pitti Palace.

In 1659, the Riccardi family acquired the palace. They altered and enlarged it, almost doubling the length of the facade. In the palace, there is also the Biblioteca Riccardiana, with an entrance on Via dei Ginori, r10. It features one of the greatest library collections in the city with manuscripts purchased from Riccardo Riccardi.

In 1814, the royal family of Lorena purchased the palace. In 1871, it changed hands again. Today, the palace houses the seat of Florence's Prefettura, the official offices of the province of Florence. It has been open to the public since the early eighteenth century. It is open every day except Wednesday. There is a seven Euros entrance fee.

The Neighborhood of San Marco

The neighborhood of San Marco, north of the Duomo, and home to the Accademia and *David*, is flooded with tourists and tourist cuisine. As you head north, however, the streets widen out a bit, and there is a much more residential feel to the area. The university is also located nearby spawning several restaurants and shops in the area. To get to the San Marco neighborhood, start at the Duomo. Take Via Ricasoli to the left of the Duomo. You can stop for a gelato at Gelateria Carabe, a Sicilian ice cream parlor, Via Ricasole, 60r. Their Sicilian *brioche gelato* (ice cream sandwiches) and *cannoli* (tube-shaped fried pastry) are the best!

David by Michelangelo

Walk down Via Ricasoli for about four blocks to Via degli Alfani. On the right, you will see the Accademia di Bella Arti, an offshoot building of the Galleria dell'Accademia. It looks like an ordinary building but you will know it by the continual line waiting to enter. If you do not make reservations, the best time to get in is in the afternoon, around 3 PM. It is the home of Michelangelo's *David* as well as his other works, such as *The Prisoners*. When you see *David*, you will know why the sculpture is so famous. I am always amazed at how the blood vessels seem to throb in his arms and hands. This museum contains four of his statues originally designed for the final resting place of Pope Julius II (a Medici) even though he was never buried there. It is open from 8:15 AM to 6:50 PM Tuesday through Sunday. It closes on Monday. You can reserve tickets at 055-294-883 or on the website www.sbas.firenze.it/academia. Admission is 6.5 Euros.

Piazza San Marco

Continue walking on the Via Ricasoli until you reach the Piazza San Marco, where you will find the Church of San Marco. You can also take Bus 6 by the train station. The bus will stop in front of the Church of San Marco. The historic monastery previously belonged to the Sylvestrines. In 1418, the Sylvestrines handed it over to the Dominicans. Financed by Cosmo il Vecchio, they enlarged the church and monastery.

While at the church, make sure you visit the Museum of San Marco, which includes part of the Dominican monastery where Fra' Giovanni da Fiesole and Girolamo Savonarola resided. I suggest that you start on the tour of the church museum at the Cloister of Sant'Antonino. Next, you will find the Sala Capitolare where Fra' Angelico frescoed one of his masterpieces, the *Crucifixion*. On the first floor of the monastery, three corridors open onto the monks' cells, which are decorated with frescoes with religious scenes entirely done by Fra' Angelo and his workshop. This is, without a doubt, one of the most interesting and emotional parts of the complex.

On Via degli Alfani, many bakeries, small grocery stores, and bars line the street where you can get *schiacciatine* (a foccaccia-like bread with salt, olive oil and sometimes peppers, olives, and other savory treats on top), sandwiches, or cold *primi piatti* (pasta) at affordable prices. Some have sit-down places that do not overcharge. Because of the proximity to the university, you will also find specialized libraries, copy shops, and printing offices.

Piazza Santissima Annunziata

From the Piazza San Marco, walk down Via Cesare Battisti for a couple of minutes. You will see the Basilica Mariana della Santissima Annunziata where you will find the colonnade designed by Filippo Brunelleschi for the Ospedale degli Innocenti, a true masterpiece of Renaissance architecture. The Ospedale degli Innocenti was an orphanage where they admitted abandoned babies. The nuns took care of the babies and provided their education. When the girls reached the marriageable age of fifteen, they gave them a dowry so they could get married.

Brunelleschi designed the orphanage in 1419. Located behind a spacious loggia, the renaissance architect created another masterpiece. You can see a number of ceramic medallions by the Della Robbia family in the spaces between the arches. They show babies in swaddling clothes and symbolize the work of the orphanage. The great loggia forms a covered walkway that is an extension of the piazza.

At the end of the loggia, at the side on the left going towards Via della Colonna, a niche houses the *ruota*, the wheel into which unwanted babies were placed. Above, look for a moving inscription in Latin taken from Psalm XXVI: "Pater et mater reliquerunt nos, Dominus autem assumpsit." It means, "Our father and mother have forsaken us, the Lord has taken us in." In addition to the Renaissance cloisters, and the beautiful eighteenth century church inside the Ospedale, an interesting collection of paintings hangs on the church walls. These include the *Adoration of the Magi*, a work painted in 1488 by Domenico.

Leave the piazza on Via del Servi. Stop at the Robiglio pastry shop, Via dei Servi, 112, one of the best in Florence. Via del Servi will take you back to the Duomo.

The Neighborhood of Piazza Repubblica

Piazza Repubblica is located a few blocks from the Duomo down Via Roma by the Baptistry. Near the corner with Via Strozzi, you will find one of the oldest and most famous grocery stores. The shop is little and there are only two or three little tables, but you should try their great rolls with truffles. You can also reach the Piazza Repubblica from Via Tornabuoni three blocks down on Via degli Strozzi, past the Palazzo Strozzi. The Florentines rebuilt the piazza in the eighteenth century enlarging the ancient market square. Many famous bars line the piazza. Le Giubbe Rossa (the Red Jackets) is a great restaurant. The waiters wear red jackets or vests. It is cheaper inside where magazines and books are available. Sometimes there are little concerts. From the Piazza Repubblica, walk down Via Calziaoli to Migone's, 85-87r, a wonderful candy store where you can find beautiful Italian candies such as panforte, riccarelli, and sugared almonds. They wrap everything beautifully in Florentine paper. They close on Sunday and Monday. On Via Calziaoli right across from the piazza, you will find Rinascente, a real Italian department store. It has four stories and has an elevator.

Loggia del Porcellino

Down Via Calziaoli you will find the Loggia del Porcellino, also known as the Loggia del Mercato Nuovo. Underneath the Loggia del Porcellino, you will see the marble wheel that commemorates the place where the *carroccio* was left, an emblem of the Florentine Republic. A *carrocchio* was a four-wheeled war altar drawn by oxen used by the medieval republics of Italy. It was a rectangular platform on which the standard of the city and an altar were erected; priests held services on the altar before the battle and the trumpeters encouraged the fighters to the battle.

Giovanni Battista del Tasso built the Loggia in the middle of the sixteenth century as a market place to sell fabrics and other items. A tourist market fills one side. The vendors sell leather bags, silk scarves, straw hats, and other arts and craft objects. On the other side, a new palace, Borsa Merci, catches your attention. The city reconstructed it after the bombing in World War II. In front of the new palace, you can stop and touch the *porcellino* (piglet). It is a bronze copy of the marble statue of a wild boar by Petro Tacca (1612). It is part of the fountain on one side of the market. The original is in the Uffizi Gallery. If you touch the snout, you will have good luck; if you throw a coin in the mouth, and it falls down into a grate, you will return to Florence.

Palazzo Davanzati

From the market place, go back one block to Via Portarossa. Go left on Via Pontarossa and you will find the Palazzo Davanzati, a private five-story palace with a stone gate. The museum depicts life in an old Florentine home. It is open daily from 8:15 AM to 1:30 PM. The admission is free.

Now walk down Via Pontarossa to Via Tornabuoni. Here is the Palazzo Bartolini. Baccio D'Angelo built it between 1517 and 1520. The city restored the palace in 1962. While D'Angelo built the palace, the Florentines complained about the architect's work saying that it had too many Roman elements. Baccio responded by inscribing, in Latin, "Carpere promptius quam imitati" above the door. Those words mean, "It is easier to criticize than to imitate."

Santa Trinita Basilica

When you reach Via Tornabuoni, by a triangular square, you will see the Santa Trinita Basilica built around 1050. They enlarged the basilica in 1300. In the piazza, you will see the Justice Column that comes from the Caracalla Baths in Rome. In 1560, Pope Pius IV gave this column to Cosimo I, a Medici ruler. He placed it in this square at that time to celebrate his victory over rivals. Buontalenti designed the elegant facade of this church. Inside the church, you will see beautiful frescoes by Lorenzo. They depict many of the occurrences during the time of Christ. The church contains many tombs and a large crypt. From here, you can take Via Borgo Santi Apostoli. The street becomes a little square with a little church, Santissimi Apostoli in Piazza del Limbo. The people buried children here. They painted a beautiful ceiling between 1100 and 1300. The church had a major restoration between 1930 and 1938. The Nazis heavily bombed this area during World War II. The Florentines rebuilt many of the buildings in their original size. From this area, you can walk down to visit the Ponte Vecchio.

The Neighborhood of Piazza della Signoria

If you do not want to walk, you can ride the bus to Piazza della Signoria: A.T.A.F. 23, A, or B

Palazzo Vecchio

Palazzo Vecchio

From the Piazza Repubblica, you walk down Via Calzaioli where you will find many shops selling all manner of goods. In a few minutes, you will reach the Piazza della Signoria, the political center of Florence. The focal point of the piazza is the imposing Palazzo Vecchio (also known as the Palazzo della Signoria). This palace once housed the government of the city of Florence. They have enlarged the palace several times over the centuries. Arnolfo di Cambio (the same architect who designed the cathedral) created the palazzo in 1294. The section not used in the museum retains its function as the offices of the Town Council. The second internal courtyard houses the only public baths in the city center. You can visit the museum inside that has some beautifully painted walls, but you may want to save your Euros for the Uffizi and Pitti Palace. You can go in as far as the inner courtyard before you have to purchase a ticket.

Loggia dei Lanzi

On the Piazza della Signoria, you will see the Loggia dei Lanzi, originally a public meeting place that is now an open-air museum. Here you can view several sculptures by Giambologna (*Rape of the Sabines*) and Baccio Bandinelli (*Hercules and Cacus*). Besides this, you will find the *Fountain of Neptune* by Bartolomeo Ammannati and the equestrian monument to Cosimo I, by Giambologna. A nineteenth century copy of Michelangelo's magnificent *David* stands in front of the palace gates.

At this point, you have a choice. You can either visit the Galleria degli Uffizi that has one of the most important art collections in the world or relax at an open-air café, e.g. the Rivoire that is famous for its hot chocolate with cream.

Before you cross the Ponte Vecchio, you will see the Galleria degli Uffizi. I prefer to visit the Uffizi on a separate day because you may want to spend most of the day there. If you are in line by 8 AM, you will not have a long wait. You can also purchase tickets ahead of time for a shorter line.

Galleria degli Uffizi

The Uffizi Gallery occupies the top floor of the u-shaped Palazzo degli Uffizi near the Arno River. Giorgio Vasari designed the museum in 1560 to hold the Uffizi (administrative offices) of the Medici Grand Duke, Cosimo I (1519-74). Later, the Medici installed their art collections here, creating what was Europe's first modern, public museum in 1591. The *Birth of Venus* and *Primavera* by Sandro Botticelli (1445-1510) and the *Madonna of the Goldfinch* by Raphael (1483-1520) will amaze even the untrained eye. Other famous works are *Doni Tondoby* by Michelangelo, *A Self-Portrait as an Old Man* by Rembrandt (1606-69), *Venus of Urbino* by Titian, and the splendid *Bacchus* by Caravaggio.

The least crowded time to visit is before 8 AM or late in the afternoon. Tickets are ten Euros. For three additional Euros, you can reserve advance tickets by phone or in Florence, you can buy tickets at the Uffizi reservation booth at least one day in advance of your visit.

Vasari Corridor

When Cosimo I, Grand Duke of Florence, traveled to work in Palazzo della Signoria (Palazzo Vecchio) from his home one mile away in the Palazzo Pitti, he worried about the dangerous dark street. Because the Medici already had experienced assassination attempts, his architect, Giorgio Vasari, designed the elevated skyway so he could travel back and forth unrecognized. They called the skyway the Vasari Corridor and it now displays a gallery of portraits from the Renaissance Era to present day. Access is only available for groups of fifteen or more. Admission is limited to certain times of the year. One look up the huge staircase was enough for me to enjoy it through photos! Admission is 28.50 Euros.

Ponte Vecchio

View of the Ponte Vecchio

The Ponte Vecchio (Old Bridge) is a famous landmark in Florence. It crosses the Arno River near the Uffizi Gallery. The Florentines built the bridge of stone pillars and wooden planks in Roman times. In 1933, a flood destroyed the bridge. They rebuilt it twelve years later. The bridge is very interesting because shops line the sides of the bridge. Originally owned by the Commune, the shops became privately owned in the 15th century.

The Ponte Vecchio is the only bridge not destroyed by Hitler's armies during their retreat in 1944. They have rebuilt the buildings at both ends that were destroyed. In 1966, a monstrous flood severely damaged the bridge. This flood of the Arno River in Florence killed many people and damaged or destroyed thousands of masterpieces of art and rare books. It was the worst flood in the city's history since 1557. With the combined effort of Italian citizens and foreign donors and helpers, or *Angeli del Fango* (Mud Angels), many of these fine works have been restored. Many American students came to Florence to assist in the restoration. Today, a lot of restoration work is still occurring. In a wonderful, beautiful movie, *The Best of Youth,* (in Italian with English subtitles), you can see how the flood affected Florence.

Neighborhood of Santa Croce

Walk south from the Bell Tower at the Duomo on the pedestrian-only Via dei Calzaiuoli, one of the city's main thoroughfares. It will eventually lead to the Church of Santa Croce. I prefer to take the bus to this area, but if you walk, there are other interesting sights. I also like to walk down Via del Corsi where there are many fascinating shops of leather goods, Florentine fine papers, and jewelry.

Church of Orsanmichele

Visit the church of Orsanmichele, midway down Via dei Calzaiuoli on the right at the corner of Via de' Lamberti. The entrance is to the rear. It is known for its medieval niche statues and for a lovely interior dominated by a grand fourteenth century tabernacle and a painting of the *Madonna delle Grazie* (1347) by Bernardo Daddi.

Casa di Dante

Go back to Via dei Calzaiuoli to Via Dante Aligheri. You are now in a district closely associated with the great Florentine poet, Dante Alighieri (1265–1321), author of *The Divine Comedy*. In the vicinity (corner of Via Dante Aligheri and Via Santa Marherita) you will find the Casa di Dante. This is actually not Dante's house. The family built this house in 1910 to commemorate the poet who did live in this area. In the house, a museum displays Dante relics (including various editions of *The Divine Comedy*). You will have to climb some stairs. It is open from 10 AM–4 PM Monday, Tuesday, Thursday, Friday, and Saturday.

Chiesa di Santa Margherita de' Cerchi

The Chiesa di Santa Margherita de' Cerchi is located next to the Casa di Dante. It is an ancient church dedicated to Margaret the Virgin. The church contains a fine altarpiece of the Madonna and Four Saints by Neri di Bicci. It is the church where Dante may have married Gemma Donati. It also contains several tombs of the Portinari family, to which Dante's great love, Beatrice Portinari, belonged. Dante met her when his father took him to the Portinari house for a May Day party. At the time, Beatrice was eight years old, a year younger than Dante. Dante instantly fell in love with her and remained so throughout his life even though she married another man, banker Simone dei Bardi, in 1287. They both belonged to the upper class, which arranged marriages from the time they were young. Beatrice died in June of 1290 at the age of 24. Dante continued to hold an abiding love and respect for the woman after her death, even after he himself married Gemma Donati in 1285 and had his own children. This visit inspired me to study Dante's life and to again read *The Divine Comedy*.

Bargello Museum

Go two more blocks on Via Dante Aligheri and turn right on Via del Proconsolo to the Museo Nazionale dei Bargello. This museum once housed Florence's medieval police headquarters, prison, and place of execution. Today, it houses the best of Florence's medieval, Renaissance, and baroque sculpture, as well as numerous beautiful salons devoted to the decorative arts. The Bargello faces the Piazza San Firenze. Right in the middle of the piazza, you will see Via dell'Anguillare. Go two blocks to Via Isola della Stinche to find Vivoli il Gelato, considered to be the home of Italy's best ice cream. One more block and you will be in the Piazza Santa Croce. I recommend that you come back another day to enjoy the Santa Croce neighborhood.

The Santa Croce neighborhood is known for the beautiful church, the markets, and many wonderful restaurants. You might want to plan to spend a morning, an afternoon, and an evening in this neighborhood.

Basilica di Santa Croce

The cathedral of Santa Croce is well-known for its frescoes by Giotto and others. Michelangelo, Galileo, Machiavelli, Foscolo, Gentile, Rossini, and Marconi have their tombs in here. It is often called the "Pantheon of the Italian Glories."

Cathedral of Santa Croce

The marble facade of the church is colorful and detailed. Inside you will see the frescoes and art sculptures by Donatello, Giovanni da Milano, and Benedetto di Maiano. The church has sixteen chapels. The day we were there, a visiting youth chorus sang beautiful Latin hymns that really made the church come alive. I enjoyed seeing the tombs of these famous Italian artists, inventors, scientists, and writers.

Even though many visitors do not go beyond Santa Croce Piazza, there is a wonderful neighborhood of the Sant'Ambrogio district. Take Via delle Pinzocere from the north side of the Piazza Santa Croce on the west side of the church. You will find the *Casa Buonarotti* at Via Ghibellina, 70r. The family of Michelangelo built this museum in the seventeenth century to show the works of Michelangelo. It contains several of Michelangelo's earlier works such as *Madonna of the Stairs* and *Battle of the Centaurs*. Michelangelo's family constructed a beautiful house that preserves much of the history of Michelangelo. It has remained unchanged over three centuries except for moments of decline and rebirth.

Sant'Ambrogio Market

Walk east from the museum on Via Ghibellina and turn left on Via dei Macci. You will find a highly recommended pizzeria on Via dei Macci, 113r called Il Pizzaiuolo. Make reservations at 055-241171. It is open every day except Sunday. Lunch is served 12 PM–3 PM and dinner from 7:30 PM–11:30 PM. A short way up on the right is the Sant'Ambrogio market, the focus of an increasingly chic neighborhood of cafés. This market is both indoor and outdoor. It is located in Piazza Ghiberti and Piazza Sant'Ambrogio. Here you will discover fresh fruits and vegetables, clothes, flowers, shoes, and house wares. Go inside if you are searching for fresh meat or fish, pasta, general groceries, or good cheeses. If you are hungry, go to the good, inexpensive restaurant inside. The market is open every weekday, except Sunday, from 7 AM-2 PM. It is near the intersection of Via della Mosca and Via de' Neri, Santa Croce.

Places to Eat in Santa Croce Neighborhood

Santa Croce is famous for its many restaurants and its nightlife.

Cibrèo Trattoria

This little trattoria, known to locals as Cibreino, shares its kitchen with the famed Florentine culinary institution that also shares its name. They share the same menu, too, though Cibreino's is much shorter. Start with the *gelatina di pomodoro* (tomato gelatin) liberally laced with basil, garlic, and a pinch of hot pepper, and then sample the justifiably renowned *passato in zucca gialla* (pureed yellow-pepper soup) before moving on to any of the succulent second courses. Save room for dessert, especially the chocolate tarts. To avoid sometimes agonizingly long waits, come early (before 7:00 PM) or late (after 9:30 PM). They do not accept reservations. They do not take credit cards. It closes on Sunday and Monday and in late July to early September.

Address: Via dei Macci 118, Santa Croce, Florence, 50121
Phone: 055/2341100

Da Rocco

At one of Florence's biggest markets, you can grab lunch to go or eat at one of the booths. The wine is *da consumo,* which means they charge you for how much you drink from the straw-colored flasks. The menu changes daily. The prices are great and the service is fast. They do not accept reservations. They do not take credit cards. They do not serve dinner. They close on Sunday.

Address: In Mercato Sant'Ambrogio, Piazza Ghiberti, Santa Croce
Phone: No phone

Danny Rock

Danny Rock is one of the few hamburger spots in Florence. There is a bit of everything at this restaurant, which is always hopping with Italians eager to eat well-made cheeseburgers and fries or one of the many tasty crepes. You can also find a basic plate of spaghetti as well as a good pizza here. It looks like an old diner with its green metal tables with matching chairs. The main dining room has a big screen showing Looney Tunes.

Address: Via Pandolfini 13r
Phone: 055/2340307

Antico Noe

The atmosphere is like an American diner, not typical of Florence. The short menu at the one-room eatery relies heavily on seasonal ingredients picked up daily at the market. The menu comes alive particularly during truffle and artichoke season (don't miss the grilled artichokes if they're on the menu). Locals rave about the *tagliatelle ai porcini* (pasta with mushrooms) and the fried eggs liberally laced with truffle. Ask for the menu in Italian, as the English version is more limited. The short wine list has some great bargains. It closes Sundays and for two weeks in August.

Address: Volta di San Piero 6r
Phone: 055/2340838

Benvenuto

Go between Palazzo Vecchio and the Uffizi to Via dei Neri. Walk a few blocks to Via della Mosca. At this Florentine institution, beloved for decades by locals and Renaissance scholars alike, the service is great, the menu long, and the food simple, Tuscan, and tasty. The list of primi and secondi is extensive, and there are daily specials as well. Do not miss the *scaloppini al Benvenuto* (veal cutlets with porcini mushrooms). It closes Sunday.

Address Via della Mosca, 16 r
Phone: 39 055 214 833

La Mucca sul Tetto

The name means "Cow on the Roof." The menu, which changes every few weeks, features Tuscan seasonal classics, as well as some unusual, tasty variations. This is a good place for *coccoli* (fried, coin-size discs of dough) served with *stracchino* (a soft, mild cheese) and prosciutto on the side. Their *bistecca alla Florentina* is fried. They also offer cooking classes. It is closed Sunday. They do not serve lunch. To get there, at the end of the Santa Croce Piazza furthest from the church, take a right on to Via Guiseppe Verdi and turn left onto Via Ghibellina.

Address: Via Ghibellina, 134r
Phone: 055/2344810

Pallottino

If you are looking for classic Tuscan food, you will enjoy their *pappa al pomodoro* (bread and tomato soup) and *peposa alla toscana* (beef stew laced with black pepper). The menu changes frequently to reflect what is seasonal; the staff is friendly, as are the diners who often share a table and, eventually, conversation. They also do pizza here, as well as great lunch specials. It closes on Monday and two to three weeks in August. It is near Vivoli Il Gelato.

Address: Via Isola delle Stinche 1r
Phone:055/289573

The Neighborhood of Oltrano (Santo Spirito)

This neighborhood is the longest walk from the apartment. You may want to take the bus: ATAF 11, 36, 37, B, C, or D.

Walk toward the Ponte Vecchio, characterized by the numerous jewelry shops. Shops of butcher and leather makers originally lined the river. When you cross this famous bridge, you arrive in an area known as the Oltrano. The area is more formally known as Santo Spirito and today has unique artistic characteristics that distinguish it from other parts of the city. During the summer, it is not difficult to find locals sitting on chairs in front of their apartment buildings, chatting and discussing the day's events. This has always been an area where many artists have lived and worked, something that is still quite visible today with the numerous restoration and art studios that line the streets. Shortly after crossing the bridge, on the left, you will see the Chiesa di Santa Felicita, Florence's oldest church, restored in the eighteenth century.

Palazzo Pitti

Up a bit further on Via de Guiciardini, a large inclined piazza leads to the entrance of the Palazzo Pitti, originally a residence of the Pitti family who went broke constructing and decorating it to outdo the Medici. The Medici eventually purchased it in 1565 to save Luca Pitti from impending debt.

In 1919, the King of Italy decided to give Palazzo Pitti to the nation so that it could be turned into a museum. One hundred-forty rooms are now divided into five different galleries: the *Galleria Palatina* (Palatine

Gallery), the *Galleria del Costume* (Costume Gallery), the *Galleria de Arte Moderna* (Gallery of Modern Art), The Royal Apartments, and the *Museo degli Argenti* (Silver Museum). The *Galllleria Palatina* exhibits over one thousand Renaissance paintings donated by the Royal Family. The *Galleria del Costume* exhibits gowns from the Medici era to modern ballroom gowns donated by current socialites. The *Galleria de Arte Moderna* exhibits contemporary work influenced by the European schools 1794-1924.

It closes the first and last Mondays of the month and on major holidays. An inclusive ticket is 11.5 Euros. It opens at 8:15 AM and closes at 4:30 PM. in winter and 6:30 PM in spring to fall. It opens at 7:30 AM in July and August. I must warn you that there are over two hundred steps in the palace. There is an elevator (*ascensore, per favore!*) but you will have to ask for it. It is down a hallway out of sight of the entrance.

Boboli Gardens

Today the palazzo houses five museums, but if you don't want to stay cooped up indoors and the weather permits it, it is strongly suggested that you visit the Boboli Gardens which is accessible from the palace's courtyard although a pretty steep climb! The extensive gardens go from the hills to the Forte Belvedere, a fortress of the city; however, if you cannot make it to the top, walk among the trees and sit on the benches to enjoy the beauty of the gardens.

Inside this garden lies the Buontalenti Grotto (1583-1593). Decorated with Mannerist-style scenes from Greek and Roman mythology, the grotto includes copies of Michelangelo's famous Slave series, the originals of which were transferred to the Galleria dell'Accademia. In the Grotto, you will find statues and sculptures created for the entertainment of viewers. One is the grotesque statue of Bacchino sitting on a turtle, created in 1560 by Valerio Cioli da Settignano. It is a satirical version of the most famous dwarf of the Medici court, Pietro Bacchino.

In the seventeenth century, the garden was extended as far as the Porta Romana. They added the Vasca d'Isola, a pond, at the center with a fountain and a statue of Neptune. In the late eighteenth century, Zanobi del Rosso built the Kaffehaus pavilion. A walk through the gardens can be strenuous as there are many steep inclines. The only way to enjoy the gardens for us senior citizens is to take our time and rest often. They do have nice restrooms and a little cafe where you can take a break.

Via Maggiore

Just outside the Piazza Pitti on the south end, you will find the splendid Via Maggio (previously known as the Via Maggiore). It is lined with gorgeous sixteenth century palaces that belonged to Florence's most noted families, not to mention all the lovely antique shops that are on both sides of the road. Shopping here is really élite, reserved for those who can afford to buy an expensive villa or an expensive Renaissance Era piece of furniture. There are also more affordable shops in the area where you can find items to bring home as souvenirs.

Casa Guidi

At the corner of the Via Maggio and the Via Romana, in the Piazza San Felice, close to the Palazzo Pitti, you will see the Casa Guidi, the former residence of poet, Robert Browning, and his wife, Elizabeth Barrett Browning. They lived here from 1847 to 1861. It is only open on Monday, Wednesday, and Friday from April 1 to November 1, 3:00 PM-5:00 PM. You ring the bell to gain entry. The residence is furnished with flea market finds that are typical examples of the nineteenth century style.

Santo Spirito Church

Walking down the narrow streets that characterize this area, you will find yourself in front of the Chiesa di Santo Spirito. If you walk down Via Maggio to Via di Santo Spirito, just go left two blocks to Via Coverelli. This will take you to the Church of Santo Spirito. It was Brunelleschi's last architectural triumph. In front of the church, every morning, they hold different markets; once a month they hold an antiques market. There are plenty of choices for dining in this area: bakeries, grocery shops, and small, family-run trattoria with homemade meals and outstanding menus at affordable prices.

Chiesa di Santa Maria del Carmine

From the Church of Santo Spirito, you can take Via Sant' Agostino that runs into Via Santa Monaca to the Chiesa di Santa Maria del Carmine, even if it is just to see the chapel of Felice Brancacci that he commissioned from Masaccio around 1420. The frescoes are truly a masterpiece of Early

Renaissance art. The entrance to the chapel is from the piazza, on the right side of the church.

If you are hungry, stop at Trattoria del Carmine, Piazza del Carmine, 18r on the corner at Borgo San Frediano. It is a family run trattoria with a traditional homey kitchen. Also, if you are a chocolate lover, plan to be here after 4:30 PM to visit the Hemingway at Piazza Piattelllina 9r. It is open from 4:30 PM–1:00 AM Monday to Thursday and 2:00 PM–1:00 AM on Sundays. Another interesting place is La Dolce Vita. It is like a huge warehouse and always crowded with the party crowd. In the evenings, it is a little wild for me, but I like to watch the people who go to have a wild time. It is in the Piazza del Carmine.

You can now return across the Arno River taking Plaza del Carmine to Borgo San Frediano across the Ponte del Carraia (a bridge.)

Places to Eat in the Oltrano Neighborhood

La Casalinga

Caslinga translates as "housewife." This place has the nostalgic charm of a 1950's kitchen with Tuscan comfort food to match. Their *ribollita* (thick peasant soup) is the best in Florence. The decor is cluttered with paintings and the tables are close together to accommodate the crowds. They have a huge menu and the portions are large.

Address: Via Michelozzi 9r
Phone: 055/218624

Osteria Antica Mescita San Niccolò

Next to the church of San Niccolò, this Osteria serves simple Tuscan food including the *cinghiale con aromi* (wild boar stew). They are closed on Sunday and in August.

Address: Via San Niccolò 60r,
Phone: 055/2342836

Neighborhood of Piazza Michelangelo

Piazza Michelangelo offers one of the most famous views of Florence. You have several ways to go there: by bus (nr 13 or nr 12) or walking from Piazza Poggi (left side of the Arno). This is a nice but fairly strenuous walk on an uphill road. It crosses a fascinating green area for those used to walking uphill for miles every day! I strongly suggest the bus. As it is a famous place, it is always overcrowded with tourists.

If you visit Florence in April to May, you may also visit the Rose Garden (free entrance). The entrance is on the right before arriving in Piazza Michelangelo. You can buy a drink in one of the bars of Piazza Michelangelo; and then, you can sit on a bench in the Rose Garden in front of an amazing panorama among roses of every color and kind. In the spring, you can also visit the Iris Garden, on the opposite side of the Rose Garden. The entrance is not free, but you can admire many irises of incredible colors. The white iris on a red background, also known as fleur-de-lis, is the symbol of Florence.

There are several bars here: all of them are a little expensive; but, if you like to sit in front of one of the most famous panoramas of the town, you can sit at the La Loggia-Caffè which is the best one (and quite probably the most expensive).

Behind the Loggia-Caffè, long stairs lead up a hill named Monte alle Croci and to the church of San Salvatore al Monte (1499). I usually take a long rest before attempting this part of the stroll! On the top of the hill, there is San Miniato that, together with the Baptistery, is the most important Romanic building in Florence. On one side of the church, you find the Vescovi Palace (1295-1320), which is part of a monastery. On the left side, you find the Monumental Cemetery where many important Florentines are buried.

Outside of Florence

There are two interesting places outside of the Florence city limits. One is The Medici Villas and the other is Fiesole.

Medici Villas

The Medici Villas are a series of rural building complexes near Florence which were owned by members of the Medici family between the fifteenth and the seventeenth centuries. The villas served several functions. They were the country palaces of the Medici, scattered over the territory that they ruled, demonstrating their power and wealth. They were also recreational resorts for the leisure and pleasure of their owners; and, they were the center of agricultural activities on the surrounding estates.

The best way to see the Medici Villas is by a tour at www. florencetour. com. They will accommodate any size group. We were met at our apartment by an eight-passenger van (for three people!). It is a little pricey (120 euro each) but well worth it unless you are up to some very long walks and bus rides. We visited the Villa Petraia and its gardens, Villa Castello (garden only as the villa inside is private), and Villa Poggio. It was a seven-hour tour with a stop for lunch (at your own expense). The guide explains everything in English.

Villa Petraia

Originally a castle of the Brunelleschi family, the Villa of Petraia became a possession of Grand Duke Ferdinand I. In 1575, under the orders of the Grand Duke, Buontalenti redesigned the villa. It has a beautiful inner courtyard covered by a glass roof. There is a series of seventeenth century frescoes by Volterrano. The villa has a series of "period" rooms furnished with beautiful paintings, pictures, and furniture. King Victor Emanuele II used the villa as his summer residence. This magnificent villa overlooks an Italian style garden designed by Tibolo.

Villa Castello

In the fourteenth century, they called this villa Il Vivaio or the Greenhouse. When the Florentines banished the Medici family, they destroyed the villa. However, Cosimo the Great commissioned Giorgio Vasari to rebuild it in a classical Renaissance design.

Currently the villa houses the Accademia della Crusca, a private school and museum. Hence, it is only possible to visit the gardens. These gardens are very beautiful and among the most magnificent and ornate in the whole of Europe.

Villa Poggio

Lorenzo the Magnificent, Grand Duke of Florence, lived in this villa during the summer. It remained the summer residence of the Medici family for centuries. Francesco I and his famous mistress, Bianca Cappello, were found dead here in 1589; they believed they were poisoned by the Grand Duke's power-hungry brother.

During the first years of the unified Italian Monarchy in the nineteenth century, the villa became the royal residence. Later on, during the Second World War, residents of the town took shelter in the villa's basement as protection from the bombing.

Fiesole

The second place is Fiesole. Take bus #6 from the train station to the Piazza San Marco. Then take bus #7. In about fifteen to twenty minutes, you will be up in the hills outside of Florence at a beautiful site called Fiesole. The bus will stop at Piazza Mino. It is encircled with cafes, restaurants, and shops. Often they will have arts and crafts fairs on Sunday. Around the piazza are some of the town's most important buildings: the Palazzo Vescovile (Bishop's Palace), originally built in the eleventh century; the town's cathedral, the Cattedrale San Romolo, constructed and enlarged between the eleventh and fourteenth centuries (It contains some fine frescoes); Palazzo Pretorio, the seat of the town council; and, the early Chiesa di Santa Maria Primerana.

The Hotel Aurora has a very nice restaurant, down some steps, with a great view of Florence. I love to go there for lunch to enjoy the view of Florence and the ambience of the terrace. You can walk over to the Cattedrale di San Romolo built in the eleventh century. Near the cathedral, you will find the Etruscan ruins. Fiesole is famous for its archaeological area that includes a B.C. Roman amphitheater, baths, and Etruscan ruins. It is closed on Tuesday. It is interesting to walk through, but you do have to walk up and down some hills. Down the road, the luxurious Villa di Maiano estate was the setting for the film, Room with a View.

CHAPTER 8:
Other Things To Do in Florence

Cooking Class and Wine Tasting

The best deal is the Accidental Tourist cooking class. You can reach them at www.accidentaltourist.com. Our guide was Steve Woodbury. Besides being a wonderful guide, he is also a beautiful singer of Italian opera. It is 100 Euros per person (about $130–$140), but it is one of the least expensive of the all day tours. I think it was worth it: transportation to the Chianti Rufina countryside, a wine tasting and tour of the winery with wine, bread and olive oil, a tour of the olive processing facility, a cooking class where you make pasta from scratch, and a delicious lunch in an 800-year-old farmhouse.

Tel: 39 055 699376 or 39 348 6590040
Website: www.accidentaltourist.com

To get to the pickup point, cross Ponte Vecchio to get on the side of the river opposite of the Uffizi. We took the bus that stops by the Uffizi Gallery. Turn left and walk along the river (with the river on your left). Shortly you will walk by the bridge, Ponte all Grazie. Ten more steps and you are in Piazza Demidoff, a square with trees and a statue in the middle.

If you run late or get lost, please call them at 348 6590040. They only accept payment in Euros because of the variations in exchange rate. You pay at the end of the tour. You can cancel this reservation by phone (phone number 055 699376) or by E-mail to info@accidentaltourist.com at least two days before the tour. In the message, please refer to the name and the date of the tour that you will receive with your confirmation

We were picked up at the Piazza Demidoff and driven through the beautiful Tuscan countryside to Rufina. First, we had a tour through the olive oil production housed in the enormous villa. Then we had a tour through the winery with explanation of the wine production process including the different recipes for wine and the aging process. After a wine tasting with delicious bread and olive oil, we again boarded the van and went to an 800-year-old farmhouse. On the ground floor is an ancient kitchen where we made pasta from scratch. We then went upstairs for a delicious four-course feast with more wine provided by the woman who lives there. Her homemade gelato is unforgettable! It was an extraordinary day.

Art Classes

I found an excellent private art studio called Isabelle Art Studio. It is north of the Mercato Centrale on Via Zanobi, 114r. You can request classes in different media at jeanne_isabelle@yahoo.fr. or www.painting-courses-florence.com. She charged sixteen Euros for a ninety-minute class. It is a small studio with about seven to eight students in the evenings. Her cell phone is 39 349 5311219. She was trained at the Sorbonne in Paris. She speaks Italian, French, and fairly good English. We had a great time learning how to use pastels, and we created two pieces of art in five lessons.

CHAPTER 9:
Eating In Florence

Italy is all about eating! In this chapter, I will tell you about eating in Florence. Many cities in Italy have their own specialties. Most good restaurants are off the beaten path. You can also eat at the forno (bakery) or pasticceria (pastry shop). They often have salumeria (cold cuts, cheese). When we are in Italy, we make it a habit to have gelato every day. Our favorites are dark chocolate, bacio (milk chocolate with toasted whole hazelnuts), pistacchio and noci (hazelnut).

The amazing thing about eating in Italy is that I never gain weight no matter how much pasta or how many biscotti I eat. In fact, I usually lose ten pounds a month. The reason is walking. Even with my arthritis, I walk more than I ever do at home. The other benefit is that my arthritis improves after I have been to Italy.

Apertivo

Pasta with Mussels

Apertivo, the Italian term for happy hour, is an absolute dream for budget travelers. You can buy a drink 5:00– 8:30 PM in most bars in Italy and you will have the opportunity to enjoy a complimentary buffet. Apertivo buffets range from a few bowls of potato crisps to impromptu dinners of salads, sandwiches, pastas, and pizza. Big apertivo buffets are especially plentiful in the Northern Italian cities of Florence and Bologna. If you buy a drink, most of them have some kind of buffet with appetizer type foods. My favorites are *crostini* (toasted bread) with chicken liver or *bruschetta*, crispy bread served with tomatoes and olive oil. They are also famous for their bell pepper spread.

Food Stands

Along the streets of Florence, you will find bars that serve food. They are famous for *lampredotto* (tripe) that I personally can live without. I love their roast pork, grilled sausage, and *panini* (boiled roast beef sandwiches*).*

Rosticceria

A *rosticceria* that specializes in roasted meat is also very popular. In the *rosticceria*, you can order to go or to eat in. They serve roasted potatoes, chicken, and skewered meat. I like their *crochete di patate* (crispy fried potatoes). Down the street from the Pitti Palace, try La Marguerita in Piazza S. Felice. They serve serve heaps of roast meats all with sides of potatoes and vegetables.

Trattoria

A trattoria is an Italian-style eating establishment, less formal than a *ristorante* (restaurant), but more formal than an osteria. There are generally no printed menus, the service is casual, wine is sold by the decanter rather than the bottle, prices are low, and the emphasis is on a steady clientele. The food is modest but plentiful (mostly following regional and local recipes), and it is usually served family-style (i.e. at common tables).

Osteria

Literally, osteria means a place where the owner hosts people, but usage has narrowed the definition. Today, an osteria is a restaurant that is big, spacious, and designed for everyone. They are usually located in neighborhoods and emphasize drinking as well as dining. They are designed to be casual and comfortable. My favorite is L'Osteria di Giovanni on Via del Moro, 22r. I had been to this restaurant in 1972. When I told Giovanni this, he immediately brought out his staff to meet us. He then brought us the *pappa al pomodoro* (tomato bread soup) and *crostini* (toasted bread slices). We had the *bistecca del Fiorentina* (Porterhouse steak) that was fabulous. On another day, we had the *corniglio* (rabbit).

Chapter 10:
Shopping In Florence

Florence is a hot spot for fashion, but that does not mean tourists have to pay high prices for ready-to-wear souvenirs. In fact, quality clothing and accessories can be found for only a few Euros at a number of outdoor markets in Florence. Shopping in Florence can be a unique experience as you wander through its ancient and medieval streets, exploring the city's renowned tradition of crafts and family-run businesses. Few cities of comparable size can boast such a profusion and variety of high-quality goods.

Walking around the city you will find shops selling Italian fashion, antiques, and jewelry as well as typical Florentine crafts. Tuscany is dwarfed by Florence when it comes to shopping possibilities. However, many of the local crafts and specialties come from the many outlying towns and villages. These range from ceramics and hand-woven materials to the region's many gastronomic delicacies.

Shops usually open from 9AM to 1 PM. In the afternoon, they re-open 3:30 PM–7:30 PM, though food shops tend to open earlier in the morning and remain closed 1 PM–5 PM. Most shops are closed on Monday morning and food stores are closed on Wednesday afternoon. Almost all shops close on Saturday afternoon in summer, and shops and markets tend to close for two or three weeks around the middle of August.

Major credit cards are usually accepted in larger shops, but the smaller ones prefer cash. Travelers' checks are widely accepted for payment of goods, though the rate is less favorable than at a bank. Shopkeepers and market stallholders should, by law, give you a *ricevuta fiscale* (a receipt.) If a purchased item is defective, most shops will change the article or give you a credit note, as long as you show the receipt. Cash refunds are uncommon.

Visitors from non-Euro countries can reclaim the twenty per cent sales tax (IVA) on purchases from the same shop exceeding 160 Euros. Ask for a *la fattura* (an invoice) when you buy the goods and inform the shop of your intention to reclaim the tax. You will need to show your passport and the shop will fill out and stamp a form that can be taken to the relevant office at the airport.

The city's main chain store is Coin, a popular independent department store. This store stocks mid-range casual clothing, shoes, toiletries, children's clothing, and toys. You will also find a huge range of fashion accessories, including hosiery, sunglasses, bags, and scarves. It has an extensive home collection. The store is located at Via dei Calzaioli, 56 r, a few blocks past the Battistero by the Duomo. A store called Rinascente in Piazza della Repubblica has designer clothing, lingerie, household items, and a rooftop bar with direct views of the Duomo. The other main department store, Oviesse, is located on Via Nazionale by the Mercato Centrale.

Outdoor Markets

Mercato dell Porcellini

The outdoor straw market in the *Mercato Nuovo* (the New Market) buzzes daily beneath a gorgeous multi-block loggia in central Florence. These vendors sell high-quality leather items, straw bags and hats, scarves, and wallets (not to mention those mini-David statuettes and cooking aprons!). We suggest smaller, cheaper, and easy-to-pack items. The Mercato Nuovo is located at the intersection of Via Calimala and Via Porta Rossa near the Piazza Repubblica.

San Lorenzo

Less picturesque, the outdoor market at San Lorenzo is an easier place to haggle with sellers. Expect crowds, barking vendors, the smell of leather, and a mix of quality and shoddy goods. This market is popular with tourists, locals, and pickpockets, so keep a watchful eye. It is located between the Mercato Centrale and Church of San Lorenzo,

Sant'Ambrogio

This indoor-outdoor market is located in Piazza Ghiberti and Piazza Sant'Amrogio near the Santa Croce church. They sell everything from fresh fruits, vegetables, meat, and fish to clothing and household goods. It is open everyday except Sunday 7 AM–2 PM.

Mercato delle Cascine

Parco delle Cascine is the biggest public green space in Florence, home to rich vegetation, sporting facilities, annual festivals, the Faculty of Agricultural Science, the School of Airborne Warfare, and even a couple of nightclubs. The park used to be part of a Medici estate.

The Mercato delle Cascine is in the very beautiful Parco dell Cascine. It opens each Tuesday morning (7 AM–2 PM). It is the biggest and cheapest market in town. If you are searching for fruits, vegetables, clothing, general groceries, house ware stands, antiquities, telephone cards, shoes, and whatever else you can think of, then come here. After shopping, do not forget to take a walk in the park. Take bus 17 from downtown Florence.

Mercato delle Pulci

This flea market is located in Piazza dei Ciompi. It is open 9:00 AM–7:30 PM every day. On the last Sunday of the month, they spread out into the neighboring streets. They sell old things (antiques), books, jewelry, coins, clothing, and furniture. You will find it near the Santa Croce Church. Take Borgo Allegri left near the entrance to the church.

Outlet Malls

There are many outlet stores in the Florence area offering visitors to Italy a chance to enjoy discounted prices on some of the most famous fashion names in Italy. Most of these outlets are located in the surroundings of Florence and are accessible by public transportation.

The Mall

It is open Monday to Saturday from 10:00 AM–7:00 PM. It is open on Sundays 3 PM–7 PM. Outlet stores include: Agnona, Alexander McQueen, Balenciaga, Bottega Veneta, Emanuel Ungaro, Ermenegildo Zegna, Fendi, Giorgio Armani, Gucci, Hogan, I Pinco Pallino, La Perla, Loro Piana, Marni, Salvatore Ferragamo, Sergio Rossi, Stella McCartney, Valentino, Yves Saint Laurent, and Emilio Pucci.

Getting there by train:

Take a train on the Florence to Rome main line and stop at the Rignano station. Take a taxi to the outlet stores.

Getting there by Turistic Bus:

This service is just on Fridays, Saturdays and Sundays. Buses leave from the Auto Stazione SITA, located in Santa Maria Novella Square, at 9:30 AM–2.00 PM. The price is nine Euros roundtrip. Check at the SITA bus station for up-to-date information.

Getting there by SITA Bus:

This service is available every day. Direct connection buses depart from the SITA bus station by Santa Maria Novella Monday to Saturday at 9:00 AM, 1:00 AM, and 3:00 PM. They return at 12:45 PM., 2:23 PM., 4:00 PM, and 7:15 PM. Check at the SITA bus station for up-to-date schedules. The price is about three Euros each way.

CHAPTER 11:
Venice

Venice is an island. The best time to go to Venice is in April, May, or September. It is very warm during the summer months. There are seasonal floods and high tides (alta acqua) usually in late October, November, and December. At those times, the streets and piazzas may be flooded. Some people wear boots or wrap their feet in plastic bags with rubber bands. You will hear many stories of dirty or smelly water. I was there in September and the water appeared very clean.

From Florence, you can go to Venice by train for the day or overnight. You may want to schedule three days to Venice because there is so much to see and do there. Venice has two train stations: one in Mestre and one in Venice (*Santa Lucia*). Mestre is known as a dormitory town where most of the workers in Venice live. The best place to stay is in Mestre, just outside Venice on the mainland. Hotels are much less expensive in Mestre. Most hotels in Venice range from $200-500 a night. Many have told me that it can also be very noisy at night. I like the Hotel Delfino because it has a bus stop right across the street and it is not too far from the train station, about a ten-minute walk. You can take a taxi, but we walked there in about ten minutes. When you come out of the front of Mestre train station, go to your right to the main street, Via Liberta. Walk down to the bridge to Corso del Populo. Turn left and walk down about three or four blocks. It is in a very quiet area on a nice boulevard street with a grocery store, cafes, and shops.

Hotel Delfino
Corso del Popolo 211
Mestre, Venice 30172
Phone #: 39 (041) 5321029
Fax: 39(041) 5310601
www.hoteldelfino-mestre.com
Or 1-800-expedia or expedia.com

The room rates are about $107 for a double room. We were fortunate to find a family suite with two bedrooms (four twin beds) for four of us. Continental breakfast is included. Venice is an island that you can reach in ten minutes by bus. There is a bus stop across the street from the hotel.

Take the train #9402 from Florence at the station of Santa Maria Novella to Mestre. It leaves at 9:30 AM and arrives at 11:21 AM. For the return trip, you can leave from the Venice train station, Santa Lucia, # 9425 at 6:27 PM and arrive in Florence at 8:30 PM.

On the bus from Mestre, you will arrive at the bus station in Piazza Roma. You will have to walk across a fairly steep bridge. Go over the bridge, Ponte Costituzione, to get to the Grand Canal. You will see the big train station, *Santa Lucia*, on your left. The public boats are called *vaporetti* (water buses). They run almost constantly. In front of the train station, you can buy the *vaporetto* tickets. You could also buy them at the ticket office by the bus station. The standard waterbus ticket is around six Euros, rather expensive if you are making several trips. You can save a lot of money by purchasing a one, three, or 7-day ticket. The Travel Cards are sold by hours:

12 hours - 14 Euro
24 hours - 16 Euro
36 hours - 21 Euro
48 hours - 26 Euro
72 hours - 31 Euro

The Vaporetto (Water Bus) of Venice

Remember to stamp your ticket in the yellow machines before boarding the *vaporetti*. Tickets are not sold on the boats. If you find yourself on a boat without a ticket, notify the ACTV crew immediately to avoid paying a fine. You can take the *vaporetto* up and down the canal on routes #1 and #2. There are signs at each stop naming the docks where they will be stopping. There are sixteen *vaporetto* docks along the Grand Canal.

The Grand Canal winds through the city of Venice in a large S shape, traveling from the Saint Mark Basin on one end to a lagoon near the *Santa Lucia* rail station on the other. This ancient waterway measures 3,800 meters (2.36 miles) long and ranges from 30 to 90 meters (about 100–300 feet) wide. In most places, the canal is approximately five meters (16 feet) deep. The canal is an ancient waterway, lined with over 1700 buildings that were mostly built from the thirteenth to the fourteenth centuries. There are only four bridges crossing the Grand Canal. If you need to cross the canal in other places, you can take a *traghetto* (water taxi) for around one Euro. They cross the canal at seven points between San Marco and the train station.

- Fondamente S. Lucia (in front of the train station) to Fondamenta San Simeon Piccolo
- San Marcuola to Fondaco de Turchi (by the Natural History Museum)
- Santa Sofia (near Ca'D'Oro) to Pescaria (fish market)
- Riva del Carbon to Fondamente del Vin.
- Sant'Angelo to San Toma
- San Samuele to Ca'Rezzonico
- Campo del Traghetto to Calle Lanza (near the Maria della Salute church)

The routes are clearly marked on street maps of Venice (look for straight lines across the canal). They often have yellow signs pointing to the landing when you are walking through neighborhoods along the Grand Canal.

Venice is divided into six districts: Cannaregio, San Polo, San Marco, Santa Croce, Dorsoduro, and Castello. Cannaregio is near the station. Also on the same side of the Grand Canal are San Marco and Castello. Santa Croce is across the Grand Canal from the train station and San Polo and the Dorsoduro are across the canal from St. Mark's.

There are twenty-six major churches in Venice. On my suggested itineraries, you will visit some of the most beautiful churches in Venice.

If you have the occasion to be in Venice on the first Sunday of September you will see the *Regata Historica* (ancient gondola parade) that has been held since 1274. It is a very famous parade where they bring out the ancient gondolas. The gondolas are beautifully carved and painted, and the passengers are dressed in their Renaissance costumes. The lead gondola is called Serenissima. There are also other colorful boats and rowers with dramatic music playing. It is a spectacular event. You can watch some versions of it on You Tube. It starts at about 3:00 PM and lasts for about two hours. The crowds are huge so you will want to be there early enough to find a seat along the Grand Canal. We took the *vaporetto* to San Marcuola dock and found a good place to sit by the San Marcuola Church.

In one day in Venice (which definitely is not enough time to enjoy this beautiful city), you can follow the following itinerary and see some of the major highlights. It would take more than two days to see all of this. You can choose the places you want to see.

Major Highlights

Ca'dOro

From the train station, take the *vaporetto* to the fifth stop, Ca'd'Oro. Ca'd'Oro (correctly called Palazzo Santa Sofia) is a beautiful palace turned into a museum and gallery. Ca'd'Oro is regarded as one of the most beautiful palaces on the Grand Canal. It is also called the "golden house" because of the gilt and polychrome external decorations that once adorned its walls. The architects, Giovanni and Bartolomeo Boni, built it for the Contarini family. The Contarini family provided Venice with eight Doges. Built in floral Gothic Style, it looks like a wedding cake on its façade. On the ground floor, you enter the entrance hall through a recessed colonnaded loggia directly from the Grand Canal. Above the colonnade, a balcony enclosed with columns and arches forms the principal salon. After the fall of the Venetian Republic in 1797, several notables owned the palace. A famous ballet dancer, Marie Taglioni, removed the Gothic stairway from the inner courtyard and destroyed the ornate balconies overlooking the court. In 1922, Giorgio Franchetti, its last owner, restored the stairway and balconies. He gave the palace and a rich art collection to the State. It is now open to the public. It is not the largest palace in Venice, but it is quiet and peaceful and usually not crowded with tourists. The views of the Grand Canal are worth the visit. It is open Tuesday to Sunday 8:15 AM–6:45 PM. It closes at 1:30 PM on Tuesday. Tickets are $15.00 US.

Rialto Bridge

The next stop is the area called Rialto, near the Rialto Bridge (*Ponte Rialto*). This bridge is the most ornate of the canal bridges and actually is a street lined with shops. It is always crowded with tourists. Anthony da Ponte built it in1592 and for three hundred years, it was the only way to cross the Grand Canal. It is the most beautiful and famous of the four bridges that cross the Grand Canal. The other bridges are the Accademia, the Scalzi, and the Calatrava. The Rialto is formed by two inclined ramps covered by a portico lined with shops. When Venice was a shipping capital of the Mediterranean area, huge cargo ships stopped here to unload and sell their merchandise. If you walk around the Rialto Bridge area, you will find many restaurants and shops crowded with tourists. You will find more interesting shops and less expensive restaurants if you wander around the narrow streets a few blocks from the bridge. I enjoyed just watching the gondolas and vaporetti gliding under this beautiful bridge. If you are an early riser, it is a worthwhile adventure to cross the Rialto Bridge early in the morning to see the open-air fish and vegetable markets in Campo del Pescaria. During the day, thousands of tourists crowd the bridge.

Piazza San Marco

One of the charms of Venice is the number of unique neighborhoods throughout the island. From the Rialto Bridge, you can cut across the San Marco district by foot to the Piazza San Marco or take the *vaporetto* around the curve of the S-shaped canal. If you can or like to walk, it is worth the walk to see the many little bridges and gondolas as you pass by the side canals. We found a nice café on a canal where we enjoyed watching those handsome gondoliers sailing by! If you like to shop, you will find many shops less expensive than on the Rialto Bridge or Grand Canal.

The Piazza San Marco or Saint Mark's Square is a large plaza with some of the most famous and beautiful buildings in Venice. All of the most important religious and civil ceremonies have always been held in this marble plaza. The most exquisite buildings in Venice surround it. There are orchestras playing day and night. It is famous for the many pigeons, but you are not allowed to feed them.

Doge's Palace

Doge's Palace is a must see but be aware that you will be climbing many huge steps throughout the building. Allow several hours and time to sit and rest in between the various sections of the Palace. The Doge's Palace is the city's most famous building. The Palace is the most representative symbol of Venice's culture. With the Basilica of San Marco at the back and the Piazzetta in the forefront, it forms one of the most famous scenes in the world. The Doge's Palace served as the Doge's residence and the seat of government. It was also the palace of justice. This was where some of the most important decisions for Venice's, and even Europe's, destiny were made. It was built in the fourth century as a castle with towers and a defensive wall. It was in a strategic position from the sea. Over the centuries, due to fires and re-buildings, it emerged as a symbol of Venetian Gothic architecture. It has the appearance of lightness from its floral decorations on the facade and the arched loggias on the sides. On the lower colonnade, the capitals are decorated with historic and biblical scenes. Outside the Doge's Palace, there is the Giant's Stairway so called because of two gigantic statues of Mars and Neptune.

Golden Staircase (Scala d'Oro)

Inside the Doge's palace, you will (slowly) climb the Golden Staircase to get to the Doge's Apartment. Sansovino designed it around 1550. Only magistrates and important people used this stairway decorated in gold stucco. Today, this apartment is noted for its magnificent painted ceilings and stone fireplaces. It has no furnishings, as they were partly stolen by Napoleon's army. You can see the opulent lifestyle of the Doges. On the second floor, you find the meeting rooms used by the highest state authorities.

The Higher Council Hall (or Sala del Maggior Consiglio)

Over two thousand members of the aristocracy met in The Higher Council Hall, on the second floor. The impressive hall, monumental in size, is remarkable not only for its incredible size, but also for the incredible beauty of its wall and ceiling decorations. Destroyed by fire in 1577, the Venetians rebuilt the hall and decorated it in splendid art. Tintoretto was the main artist. His *Paradise* is the largest oil painting in the world. Finished by his son, this painting is renowned for it mystic light. On three sides of the hall, just under the ceiling's gilt decorations, portraits of the seventy-six Doges hang on three sides of the hall under the ceilings' gilt decorations. They sum up the history of Venice, including the tale of Marin Faliero, the Doge accused of high treason whose portrait is covered by a black cloth.

Hall of Compass

The Venetians held court and served justice in the Hall of Compass. It is a large room with beautiful paintings on the ceilings and walls. In the basement, you can visit the prison by going through the Bridge of Sighs. The Palace prisons were famous for being difficult to escape. However, Giacomo Casanova did manage to escape. He is a romantic Italian hero and famous adventurer. Known for his seductions, scholarship, and world travel, his celebrity occurred after his famous escape on the night of October 31, 1756. The escape has become a legend of Venice. His wooden cell, which you can visit, had a wooden plank floor that he dug up. He climbed up onto the roof and down into an attic. A guard on the Golden Staircase saw him, but the guard thought he was a politician who had been locked in. The guard let him out and Casanova fled in a gondola, after having coffee in San Marco Square!

The Bridge of Sighs

The Bridge of Sighs connects the Old Prisons of the Doge's Palace to the New Prisons located beyond the Palazzo River. The bridge of Sighs, so named by Lord Byron in the nineteenth century, was named from the sighs of condemned prisoners as they were being led to prison. They built it in the early seventeenth century, designed by Antonio Contino.

St. Mark's Basilica

When you leave the Doge's Palace, you will see the monumental structure, St. Mark's Basilica. The basilica is closed on Sunday to visitors. It took several centuries to build. It is a mixture of Byzantine, Roman, and Venetian architecture. Peter asked Mark, one the Four Evangelists (including Luke, Matthew, and John) to write his gospel. The Venetians chose him as their patron saint because of his ties with Rome and his separation from the Byzantine Church. The Venetians built the church as his tomb in 828 A.D. when two Venetian merchants stole his remains from his tomb in Alexandria. Having the remains of one of the Four Evangelists spelled prosperity for Venice. A winged lion with a sword, the symbol of St. Mark, became the symbol of Venice. The Church has five domes supported by five great arches. The beautiful mosaics capture the attention of thousands of tourists every year. The mosaic tiles lean in different directions to catch and reflect the light from all angles. It is a wonderful experience to sit in the piazza and see the glimmering mosaics in the sunset. Next to the Basilica is St. Mark's Campanile, the bell tower. It is 97 meters high topped with a golden statue of the Archangel Gabriel. In 1902, the tower suddenly collapsed. They reconstructed it because of the profound attachment Venetians had for this monument. In 1912, the statue of the Archangel Gabriel was once again in place. The tower has five bells: the Nona that rings on the ninth hour, the Marangona that rings both morning and evening to mark the working day, the Maleficio that announced those condemned to death, and the Trottiera and the Pregadi that ring to announce the beginning of the court and senate.

The best time to visit is early in the morning before the pigeons and tourists swarm every inch of the piazza. In the evening, the piazza is not as crowded and there is great entertainment by the many orchestras playing throughout the plaza. In the evenings, you will see many dancing to the beautiful music.

Art in Venice

If you going to spend more than one day in Venice, I recommend you visit at least one of the following four sites. The first three sites are all on the same side of the canal and you can go from one to the other, if you have a great desire for great art. All four will take a full day so you should stop for a nice lunch somewhere in between. Alternatively, just pick a couple to see. I am sure you will want to return to Venice in the future.

The Church of Santa Maria della Salute

This church is on the Grand Canal across from San Marco Piazza. This fabulous church was built in response to the Black Death that devastated the Venice population in 1347 and in 1630. The Venetians had promised in their prayers to the Virgin that they would build a church in her honor if they were saved from the Plague. In 1631, when the Plague ended, they built the Basilica di Santa Maria della Salute to thank the Virgin. Baldassare Longhena designed it. If you happen to be here on November 21, you will witness a yearly procession from San Marco Piazza to the Salute for a service in gratitude for deliverance from The Plague. They construct a pontoon bridge to connect St. Mark's and the Church of Santa Maria della Salute. This is a major event in Venice. The basilica's white color and outstanding architecture in Renaissance style creates a beautiful scene. The statue of *The Virgin with Child* by Le Court was placed on the altar. Next to the cathedral is the *Dogana*, or customs house, that was built in the shape of a ship's bow with a statue of a golden glove supported by giants. It is called the *Statue of Fortune.*

The Peggy Guggenheim Collection

Even if you are not interested in contemporary art, it is worth taking a little time to visit this museum just for the views from the terrace on the Grand Canal. The core mission of the museum is to present the personal collection of Peggy Guggenheim. The collection holds major works of Cubism, Futurism, Metaphysical painting, European Abstraction, avant-garde sculpture, Surrealism, and American Abstract Expressionism by some of the greatest artists of the twentieth century. These include Picasso, Duchamp,

Miró, Magritte, and Pollock. You can Google this museum and read a great biography of Peggy Guggenheim.

The Galleria dell'Accademia

The Galleria dell'Accademia is the best museum to see in Venice. It is a good idea to book your tickets in advance (go to tickitaly.com) The Galleria dell'Accademia is open seven days a week. Tuesday–Sunday, it is open 8:15 AM–7:15 PM, whereas on Monday the gallery is open 8:15 AM– 2:00 PM only. It is closed on Christmas Day, New Year's Day, and May 1. It is in the Dorsoduro District of Venice. There is a vaporetto stop near the Accademia. You will approach from the huge wooden arch of the Ponte dell'Accademia. As with any museum or gallery, planning is everything. There are twenty-four rooms in all so it is best to focus on some of the finest works. The successive rooms of the Accademia follow the history of painting in Venice in rough chronological order. I have selected ten of the finest works in the gallery that follow the same principle. If you see nothing else, focusing on these works will give you an overview of the history of Venetian art between the fourteenth and eighteenth centuries.

- *Coronation of the Virgin* by Paolo Veneziano (1310–1362)
- *The Camerlenghi Madonna* by Giovanni Bellini (1430–1516)
- *Procession of the Relinquary of the True Cross in Piazza San Marco* by Genile Bellini (1429–1507)
- *The Dream of St. Ursula* by Vittore Carpaccio (1465–1526)
- *The Tempest* by Giorgione (1476–1510)
- *Presentation of the Virgin in the Temple* by Titian (1480–1576)
- *Portrait of a Melancholic Young Man* by Lorenzo Lotto (1480–1556)
- *Miracle of St. Mark Freeing the Slave* by Jacopo Tintoretto (1519–1594)
- *The Mystic Marriage of St. Catherine* by Paolo Veronese (1528–1588)
- *Fire at San Marcuola* by Francesco Guardi (1712-1793).

While on this side of the canal you can go to see the Ca'Rezzonico at the next vaporetto stop.

Ca' Rezzonico Museum

The Ca' Rezzonico Museum is closed every Tuesday as well as on Christmas Day, New Year's Day, and May 1. It opens 10 AM-5 PM from November 1 to March 31. Otherwise, it is open until 6 PM. Tickets are 9.50 and 12.50

Euros. Seniors age 65 and over and students ages 14-29 get the reduced price. You can buy tickets there or from tickitaly.com.

The Ca'Rezzonico exposes us to life in Venice in its greatest days. The wealthy Bon family commissioned the palace to be built in 1649 in Venetian Baroque style. The cost of building this palace contributed to the financial ruin of the Bon family. In 1756, the Rezzonico family, noveau riche, finished the palace. In 1758, they commissioned Guarana, Dizani, and Tiepolo to create the frescoes that are now among the best preserved in Venice. The palace has a magnificent ballroom, marble balustrades with statuary, and a painted ceiling of Apollo riding his chariot around the globe. Ludovico Rezzonico married Faustina Savorgnan, joining two of Venice's most powerful families. The painting depicts them being drawn by Apollo's chariot. Their son was elected Pope Clement XIII in the same year.

By the early nineteenth century, this family became bankrupt. The home passed through the hands of many families, becoming the home of poet Robert Browning and his artist son, Robert Barrett Browning, in 1880. In 1935, after other owners, the house was sold to the City Council of Venice. Now, it displays Venice's vast collection of eighteenth century art. It also exhibits collections of Murano glass from the eighteenth century, period furniture, and artworks from Giambattista Tiepolo.

From Ca'Rezzonico you cross over the canal by *traghetto* to visit the Palazzo Grassi. The next stop after Ca' Rezzonico is S. Toma.

Palazzo Grassi

Giorgio Massari (1687-1766) designed this palace while he was finishing Ca'Rezzonico on the opposite side of the Grand Canal. The Grassi family, originally from Chioggia, commissioned the palace on a plot of land in a magnificent location; its trapezoidal form offered the added advantage of providing a long façade on the canal. It is believed that work began in 1740. It was completed in 1758. This was the last palazzo to be built in Venice before the fall of the Republic.

The palace had many owners until it was bought by Gianni Agnelli of the Fiat group in 1983. Following the death of Gianni Agnelli, Fiat chose to terminate its involvement. In May 2005, François Pinault decided to take over Palazzo Grassi. He hired the famous Japanese architect, Tadao Ando, who transformed the palace into a museum to display contemporary art. It is open every day from 10 AM—7 PM except on Tuesdays, Christmas Day, and New Year's Day. Tickets are fifteen Euros (about $22.00) so you should be a fan of contemporary art, although the palace is worth seeing.

Scuola Grande di Rocco

At the *vaporetto* stop, S. Toma, you can get off and walk about seven blocks to the highly recommended Scuola Grande di Rocco. It houses over sixty paintings by the city's favorite native son, Jacopo Tintoretto. Considered by many to be Venice's greatest painter, Tintoretto spent the Renaissance seeking to combine the color of Titian with the drawing skill of Michelangelo. He became the city's most revered artisan. His entire cycle of paintings took him twenty-three years to complete. The first floor is not well lighted but the next floor has great lighting where the massive paintings hang from the rafters. The color and intensity of Tintoretto's finest work are on full display. His version of *The Last Supper* is unconventional as it focuses on the gift of the Eucharist rather than Jesus interacting with Apostles.

Fun Things To Do

If you have the time, the great joy of Venice is to just walk around the city. It is a magical place. Your visit to Venice will still be wonderful even if you prefer to eliminate galleries and museums. On one trip, I skipped the traditional sites and wandered around the narrow streets and canals and rode the vaporetto up and down the Grand Canal.

Another great adventure is to go to the island of Murano to see the Venetian glassblowers. From the train station, take the DM vaporetto (*Diretto Murano*). It takes seventeen minutes to reach Murano. I was not a big fan of colored glass until I saw the beautiful pieces created on Murano. They are not cheap, but you can look for free.

One day I stopped at a grocery store and bought a picnic lunch to eat out on the docks at the Lido. The Lido is a resort island with grand hotels and beaches. Take the #1 vaporetto from a pier near San Marco. When you get off of the vaporetto, you will find the main area with shops and restaurants near the port. I have also walked through the village and enjoyed seeing the beautiful villas built in the nineteenth century. I enjoy the boat ride over and sitting in a cafe watching people from all over the world. Most of the beaches are private to the hotels. There is a public beach, but I hear the water is not too clean and the sand is hard to walk on because of the many shells. In my Golden Years, I prefer to just gaze at the beautiful water and shell covered beaches.

Gondolas

A Gondolier in Venice

Riding in a gondola is one of the magical experiences of Venice. Gondoliers line up near all of the vaporetto sites. Make sure you negotiate the price before you get on. It will cost about ninety Euros for a fifty minute ride. That is the price of the gondola ride. You can have up to six people in a gondola but four is very comfortable. If you split the price four ways it is not so expensive. Prices will be higher in the evening and you will pay extra for a serenade. The prices go up to around 120 Euro after 7 PM. A ride around sunset is very beautiful. I prefer gondola rides down the little canals away from the Grand Canal. It is very quiet and the old, colorful buildings create a wonderful ambience. Look for gondoliers near the smaller canals. The gondoliers are gallant and help us board the gondola without slipping and sliding.

Safety

As in all cities in Italy, stay alert as pickpockets are everywhere. Using your safety waistpack with locks is a great idea. As mentioned before, I always keep my passport, money, and credit cards in a neck pouch pinned to my underwear. Also, avoid the street vendors. Most of them are not from Italy, and it is actually illegal to purchase the fake merchandise. Fines can run into thousands of Euros. Most of the street vendors are from Senegal. With sales of fake goods running at four to six billion dollars a year, the Venice authorities are under pressure to enforce the law. However, it is not highly enforceable. Always check your chosen item to see where it is made. Many of the supposed Murano glass items and masks are "Made in China."

Restrooms

There are public restrooms in Venice for those of us who need relief every few hours:

San Marco: in the Calle Large dell'Ascensione, just beyond the narrow end of the Piazza San Marco. Go through the archway and you will find a sign pointing to WC.

Accademia: at the foot of the Accademia bridge on the Dorsoduro side of the Grand Canal.

Santa Lucia Railroad Station: through the cafeteria area.

Piazzale Roma: where the buses arrive in Venice.

Ca'Rezzonico: in the lobby next to the gift shop; very clean, and free even if you are not visiting the museum.

CHAPTER 12:
Milan

The airport of Milan (MXP) is named Malpensa Aeroporto. If you are flying home from Milan, I recommend that you go a day earlier and see the sights of Milan. We stayed at the Novotel Milano Malpensa Airport Hotel, Via Al Campo in Cardano al Campo. I use the website www.initalia.it. (Phone # 39 0226830102). Our superior double rooms were $115.00 per night. (Most hotels in downtown Milan cost about $200–300 per night for a double room.) The Novotel Milano Malpensa Hotel is a comfortable modern hotel with elevators, a restaurant, an outdoor patio, and a pool. They also have computer stations you can use free for fifteen minutes. The restaurant has very good food but is expensive. Our usual plan is to have our largest meals in the city and then take some fruit, drinks, or snacks to the hotel for later. There are no other restaurants within walking distance. Make sure you reserve your shuttle early because it does fill up for morning runs to the airport.

They have a free shuttle to the airport. It is about a ten-minute ride. If you stay in the downtown city of Milan, you have to get up early to get to the train station from your hotel and catch the Malpensa Express airport shuttle. In heavy traffic, the bus may take almost an hour to reach the airport. I prefer being close to the airport the night before, and then I have just a ten-minute shuttle to the airport.

We try to arrive in the afternoon two days before our flight. We arrive at the Milano Centrale train station from Florence. It is a Eurostar (you need reservations), and it takes about two and a half hours. When you arrive at the train station, exit to your left and go outside. You will find the Malpensa

Airport shuttle buses. Take the one that goes to the Malpensa airport, Terminal One. A roundtrip ticket costs twelve Euros. When you arrive at the airport, call the hotel and they will pick you up in the shuttle near Gate 7. We arrive in the afternoon and spend a relaxing evening in the hotel. The next morning we take the free hotel shuttle to the airport and catch the Malpensa Express train, to downtown Milan. Take the shuttle train inside the airport that goes to the Cadorno Station as it closer to downtown. You must buy your ticket in the airport before you get on the shuttle train: 11 Euros one-way and 14.5 Euros roundtrip. They have an information booth in the airport that can steer you in the right direction. Also, ask for a map of Milan. When you arrive at the Cadorno Station, walk to Foro Buonaparte to Via Dante. It is an open mall with sidewalks lined with designer shops and cafes. Ahead you will see the Duomo, an exquisite cathedral.

Milan's Cathedral Duomo

In white Candoglia marble, the majestic construction is about 157 meters in length and 93 meters in width. Its tallest spire reaches a height of 108 meters. There are more than 3400 statues mounted on the cathedral. It took five centuries to complete this beautiful cathedral. It was started in 1386. It is the most important work of Gothic architecture in Italy. During the construction lasting over five centuries, many architects have influenced the style. The facade was started in 1567 and was built in a classic-baroque style with a certain variety of classical and neo-gothic elements. By 1805, front works were finished, while the construction of the statues continued through the nineteenth century. The golden statue of Madonna, 108 meters in height, sits atop the roof as a symbol of Milan.

Outside the front altar of the cathedral, go around the corner and you will find an elevator to the top. There are guards there and I think you have to pay about eight Euros. It is a small elevator, not advertised, but it beats walking the 250 steps to the top. It is a stunning view at the top where you can see the exquisite architecture up close.

Milan Cathedral (Duomo)

Corso Vittorio Emanuele

Right next to the piazza of the Duomo, you will see the shopping mall, Corso Vittorio Emanuele II. It represents the most popular covered shopping street in Milan. Situated on the side of the Cathedral of Milan, flanked by modern porticoes, this walking passage offers the greatest selection of stores and boasts the second largest pedestrian precinct in the city center. It has a modern design with two glass-vaulted arcades, crossing in an octagon. Even on rainy days, Corso Vittorio Emanuele II is very convenient for shopping providing shelter and a cozy ambience for shoppers.

There is a tradition in this huge mall to find the mosaic bull in the center of the tile floor. You are supposed to turn your heel in the private parts of the bull to insure luck for the future. You will see many people doing this as they walk casually through the mall.

Milan is famous as the great fashion center of the world, even more so than Paris. Good shopping streets include Via Dante between the Duomo and the Castle. You can take the tram to Via Monte Napoleone near the Duomo. You will find very expensive and exclusive fashions in the Quadrilatero d'Oro. Further away is the Corso Buenos Aires area that has less expensive shops and chain stores. Window-shopping is fun if you do not want to empty your wallet. Although fashion was a high priority for me twenty or thirty years ago, I no longer have need for expensive and often svelte fashions. I have found that you can develop a stylish look by adding beautiful scarves and accessories to your elastic waist pants and tunics. You can walk from the Duomo apse toward Via Vittorio Emanuele to the Montenapoleone area, but it is about a mile. There are trams (electric streetcars) that run all over Milan. We had a little trouble figuring out what tram to take, but you can ask for directions. The Milanese people are friendly and helpful even though they have that "big city in a hurry" look.

Tram in Milan

The Last Supper

One of the main attractions in Milan is *The Last Supper* (*Cenacolo Vinciano*) by Leonardo Da Vinci. You must have tickets well in advance (several months) to see this masterpiece. I use the Web site, www.tickitaly.com. They send you your vouchers right away and you print them out. Do not forget to take them with you! It will cost 16 Euros for each adult. *The Last Supper* is in the church, Santa Maria della Grazie. Take tram #24 from the center of Milan. You can walk, but I think it is quite a walk. The tram will drop you off right in front of the church. They do not always give you your choice but I would request an afternoon time, so you can visit the Duomo and downtown in the morning. The Cadorno station is not too far from *The Last Supper*, but I still prefer to take the tram. You will enter at the specified time. The guides walk you through several "cleaning rooms." The chapel where you find *The Last Supper* is temperature controlled. You are only allowed fifteen minutes for viewing. It was not available for viewing for several years because of restoration. It is actually frescoed onto the wall of the chapel so it is not removable. It is a sight that you will not soon forget.

CHAPTER 13:
Rome

Rome is a very big city. It is filled with art, historic ruins, monuments, and exquisite views. It is the former capital of the Roman Empire. There is history everywhere. As they say, Rome was not built in a day. Therefore, if you really want to see Rome, you must plan to stay several days.

It is said that Rome was started by Romulus. Romulus and Remus were twins raised by a wolf-mother. Augustus was the first Emperor. Palatine Hill is the location of the archeological sites in Rome: The Colosseum and the Forum. The city extends over six other hills: Quirinale, Viminale, Esquilino, Celio, Aventino, and Capitolino. The best view from the seven hilltops is from the dome of St. Pietro (St. Peter's Basilica) and the Pincio, in the park of the Villa Borghese overlooking the Piazza del Populo.

Even though many travel books will tell you it is a walking city, I have to say you must be in very good condition to walk around this city. We went one day by train and tried to see the city on our own. We were lost most of the time and exhausted after only a few hours.

The best way to see Rome in your senior years is by limo. I use Bob's Limo. Go to www.romelimousines.com. His e-mail is bob@romelimousines. com or just Google Bob's Limos. They play *Arrivederci, Roma* while you are on the Web site. Their phone number from the United States is 1-877-666-BOBS. You can cancel with no charge if it is more than twenty-four hours before your scheduled appointment. It is expensive, about $100 each, but worth every penny. The driver will meet you at the train and depending on the number of people will take you to his Mercedes sedan or van. The driver was an excellent guide and very entertaining. I felt very fortunate not to be behind the wheel as he entered roundabouts and was surrounded by vespas (little motorcycles) at every intersection. We saw the following sites in eight hours including a leisurely lunch. It would probably take you three days to see all of this on your own. Therefore, you save on hotel expenses. He drives you right up to the sight! Next, I will describe the sights you should try to see. There are hundreds more sights to see, but you cannot see it all in a day!

You can ask your driver to take you to the sights you wish to see. We took the Eurostar train #9311 at 8:24 AM from Florence and arrived at the Roma Termini (train station) at 10:00 AM. Bob's Limo met us with our name on a sign. We returned to Florence from the Roma Termini #9450 to Florence at 6:30 PM. Our driver, Angelo, dropped us off at the train station at 6:00 p.m. We were back to Florence at 8:09 PM. Angelo is an actor and entertained us all day.

Piazza del Popolo

During the Middle Ages, Piazza del Popolo formed the main entrance to the city for pilgrims and travelers arriving on the Via Flaminia (from the north). It was only when Pope Sixtus V placed the Egyptian obelisk of Ramses II in the center of the square that Piazza del Popolo took on its current function. The obelisk is the tip of the trident formed by the three streets that begin in the square: Via del Corso, Via di Ripetta, and Via del Babuino. The architect, Valadier, designed the square in an elliptical shape. Groups of statues overlook two shell-shaped fountains.

Pincio

These lovely gardens overlook Piazza del Populo. There were gardens here even in the time of Ancient Rome, and it is said that they were quite fabulous. The architect Valadier designed the present-day gardens. He also designed Piazza del Popolo. In these gardens, Piazzale Napoleone I offers an unforgettable view of Rome, along with the famous Water Clock that dates back to the nineteenth century. Plan a visit to the restaurant, Casina Valacier, for a coffee or a light lunch. The Casina was originally a farmhouse, transformed by Valadier into a small neo-classical villa with terraces, loggias, columns, and capitals for Cardinal Della Porta. The bust of the astronomer, Angelo Secchi, stands in the small square in front of the house and, if you look carefully, you will see a small hole that indicates the point where the meridian passes through Rome. The Casina was originally built on an ancient Roman water tank whose pipes were used as a hiding place during the sacking of Rome in 1527. Now it is a fashionable café-restaurant where artists and intellectuals meet. It is reached by going up the Viale D'Annunzio and finally the Via A Mickievicz.

Villa Borghese

Villa Borghese is a beautiful garden, the second largest public park in Rome. Inside the gardens, you will find a villa that houses a museum. Flaminio Ponzio designed the garden for the Villa Borghese Pinciana. Some of the highlights of the garden are: The Water Clock, Fontana, Alpini Monument, and *La Galleria Nazionale d'Arte Modern* (The National Gallery of Modern Art).

The Spanish Steps

Piazza di Spagna (The Spanish Steps) is a steep climb of about 138 steps linking the Palazzo Monaldeschi in the piazza below, with the Trinità dei Monti, a church, above. *Piazza di Spagna* is always crowded with people. It is also a favorite location shoot for international films. It was built in the eighteenth century, and the steps have been restored several times to preserve their original state. Another advantage to the limo tour is that the driver will drive you to the top, so you do not have to climb all those steps.

Colosseum

The Colosseum in Rome

The Colosseum was built 70–82 AD. It was originally built as an amphitheater to hold spectacles such as gladiator match ups and other forms of entertainment during the Roman Empire. The Colosseum is made of cut stone and masonry. The elliptical structure can accommodate 50,000 spectators. There were eighty entry points so that the crowd could easily get in and out of the amphitheater. Today it holds concerts and special events.

The structure is huge. It has three layers of arcade, maybe to hold different events all at the same time. At times, it was filled with water to have races by boats. Of course, you know the story about the lions fighting the gladiators!

Trevi Fountain

The Trevi Fountain

Trevi Fountain is also full of tourists. People are always throwing coins and making their three wishes. It is a lovely sight. As you emerge from the narrow cobble stone streets that open into Trevi Square, you will be greeted by the breathtaking site of the Trevi Fountain, one of the largest and most beautiful statues in the world. The sculpture of the fountain appears to emerge from the walls of the building behind it.

The Trevi Fountain (*Fontana di Trevi* in Italian) is located in the heart of Rome's historic center near the Spanish Steps. The Trevi Fountain is located at the meeting of three roads (*tre vie*). The fountain was built at the end of an aqueduct (*Acqua Virgo*) that was constructed in 19 B.C. The fountain is a perfect stopping point in the middle of your tour of Rome. You can grab a bottle of water or a gelato from one of the nearby shops and then relax on the steps surrounding the fountain.

An estimated 3,000 Euros are thrown into the fountain each day. The money has been used to subsidize a supermarket for Rome's needy. However, there are regular attempts to steal coins from the fountain

The Pantheon

The Pantheon in Rome

The Pantheon is an incredible structure built about thirty years before Christ (B.C.). I would not miss the Pantheon ever. This was one of the highlights of our tour. The Pantheon is one of the best-preserved buildings. It is amazing how the ancients could build such an enormous building with ancient tools. It was originally built as a temple for all the gods. When you look up at the ceiling, you see the huge dome with the hole in the middle where rain runs down to the floor. This circular opening is known as the oculus. It provides the only light into the Pantheon. The oculus is about thirty feet across. The purpose of the oculus was not only to illuminate the interior, but it was also built to let those in the temple contemplate the heavens.

The floor of the Pantheon is slanted to let rainwater drain from the building. One of the most remarkable things about the Pantheon in Rome is that the inside dome is as high as it is wide, about 142 feet (43.3 meters). The dome is the inspiration for many domes that came later including St. Peter's dome designed by Michelangelo and the dome in Florence designed by Brunelleschi. When you stand outside in front of the Pantheon, you will see the famous Latin inscription that translates as "Marcus Agrippa, son of

Lucius, consul for the third time, built this." The first temple was indeed built by Marcus Agrippa, son-in-law of the Emperor Augustus, between 25 and 27 B.C. However, this first temple was destroyed by fire in 80 A.D.

If modern unreinforced concrete were used in a building of the size of the Pantheon in Rome, it would not stand under the load of its own weight. The composition of the concrete used in the dome is still unknown.

The entire collection of Roman gods was called the Pantheon. In ancient times, you could worship any of the gods whose statues were located in the niches in the Pantheon. Pope Boniface IV converted the Pantheon into a church to ensure the Pantheon's preservation. It is considered sinful to remove any item. Many famous Italians are buried in the Pantheon, including the Renaissance painter, Raphael, and King Vittorio Emanuele.

The Forum

The Roman Forum is a block of huge columns, an assembly of ancient buildings at the heart of Rome. This place used to be the business district during the time of Augustus. When the Roman Empire fell, the Forum was left to decay and had become a cattle pasture during the Middle Ages. What remains now are the Arch of Titus, the Arch of Septimuus Severus, and the Arch of Constantine. The Romans removed some of the stone to build churches and temples.

The Arch of Constantine

The Arch of Constantine is well-preserved. A carved frieze encircles the three archways. These reliefs depict scenes from the Italian campaign of Constantine against Maxentius which was the reason for the construction of the monument. Constantine's supporters built this arch to commemorate Constantine's victory over Maxentius in 312 A.D.

The Vatican Museum

The Vatican Museum was another highlight of our trip. You can book your tickets online to avoid the long queues. Once again, the advantage of the limo driver is that he finds out when the line is short and takes you there then. We did not have to wait at all!

The entrance to the Vatican Museum is by the "Stairway to Heaven" which is actually a huge ramp that spirals up forever. We called it the "Stairway of Pain." To see the Sistine Chapel, you must go through the whole museum, which is beautiful, but we found it rather exhausting. The rooms on the way have beautiful tapestries and gold ceilings embellished with hundreds of frescoes. By the time we arrived at the Sistine Chapel, we almost forgot where we were going. The hall is rather dark and crowded. Of course, you will have a stiff neck from looking up at the beautifully painted ceiling. I purchased a book in the bookstore that beautifully illustrates the segments of Michelangelo's story of the Creation. From the first time I visited the Sistine Chapel, when I was twenty-five, I do not remember the exhausting entrance. The next time I go to Rome, I think I will sit in the piazza and look at my book!

The Stairway to Heaven is the entrance to the Vatican Museum

The Palatine Hill

The Palatine Hill is located between the Circus Maximus, the Colosseum, and the Roman Forum. It is one of the most famous of the seven hills in Rome. Much of the hill is now an excavation site; the most recent discovery is the Lupercal Cave.

Like most of the historical architecture scattered in Rome, the Palatine Hill was home to opulent palaces and buildings of the Roman Empire like those belonging to Cicero, Augustus, and Marc Anthony. They all had homes on the Hill. What remains now are the preserved ruins of the dated structures and a beautifully manicured garden. It is still a spectacular landscape. Our driver drove us right up to the sight and saved us from a lot of walking.

Vittorio Emanuele II Monument

The Majestic Monument of Vittorio Emanuele II

It is an imposing monument built in 1885–1911 to celebrate the fiftieth anniversary of the unification of Italy, in 1861. It is so tall you can see it from all over Rome. It is made of white marble. Winged lions and two bronze statues of the goddess Victoria, driving a quadriga (a chariot pulled by four horses), flank the enormous flight of steps. The gigantic statute of King Vittorio Emanuele II rising on a horse resides in the middle of the monument. The monument is designed with Corinthian columns almost fifty feet high. Do not try to sit on the steps or a guard will admonish you!

Piazza Navona

This large piazza is famous for its Bernini fountains: The Fountain of the Four Rivers (1651) with an obelisk, the Fountain of Neptune, God of the Sea, and the Fountain of the Moor. The rivers in the Fountain of the Four Rivers represent the Danube, the Ganges, the Nile, and the Rio de la Plata. The piazza is surrounded by cafes.

Via dei Condotti

Via dei Condotti, a famous street of designer shops, begins at the Spanish Steps. It is named after conduits or channels which carried water to the Baths of Agrippa. The Via dei Condotti dates back to the atelier, Bulgari, a jeweler and maker of luxury goods. It opened in 1905. As you stroll down the street (most likely window shopping!) you will see Valentino, Armani, Cartier, Louis Vuitton, Gucci, and Prada. There are many cafes and restaurants along the street, a nice place to people watch. As it is near the Spanish Steps, large numbers of tourists and Italians crowd the streets. In 1989, the fashion designer, Valentino, went to court and attempted to stop McDonald's from opening near the Spanish steps, complaining of "noise and disgusting odors" in the vicinity of Via dei Condotti. To the dismay of some Romans, McDonalds did open there.

CHAPTER 14:
Day Trips

San Gimignano

The SITA bus will take you from Florence to San Gimignano in about an hour and a half. There is a connection in Poggibonsi. The bus will stop right outside the main gate (Porta del San Giovanni). From there, you can wander up and down the cobblestone streets. It has many shops and restaurants and some art museums. You must travel by foot inside the walls, but there is an inexpensive electric shuttle bus that goes all day from Porta San Giovanni to Piazza della Cisterna to Porta San Matteo.

San Gimignano is named after the Bishop of Modena, Saint Gimignano, who saved the city from the Goths. Historical evidence proves the tiny city began in 63 B.C. During the medieval era, the wealthy families, who engaged in commerce, ordered seventy-two towers built, but they could not exceed the height of the Commune tower, Rognosa.

The entrance to the medieval city, San Gigmignano

In 1199, the city became an autonomous council, freeing itself of the dominion of the bishopric of Volterra. In this era, the village suffered internal divisions between Papal-supporting Guelphs and Empire-supporting Ghibellines, who caused a real civil war in the territory. Dante Alighieri came to the city to help mediate the feuds in 1300. The plague in the mid-fourteenth century aggravated the socio-economic crisis in the village which, in 1354, accepted submission to the authority of the Florentine Republic. From that moment, San Gimignano became one of the most important centers of Tuscany, despite its obvious demographic decline. Of the 13,000 inhabitants at the beginning of the fourteenth century only 3,000 remained at the end of the fifteenth century due mostly to the Black Plague. However, those factors did not stop the construction of the town center. In recent times, the citizens of San Gimignano recognized that they owned an authentic, valuable, open-air artistic heritage. With all of its medieval structures still intact, the center has been recently added to the list of UNESCO-protected heritages.

The Piazza del Cisterna is a popular gathering place. When you enter the front gate (Porta San Giovanni), walk up the hill on San Giovanni and you will find the piazza there with an interesting old well. Try not to miss the great gelato as soon as you enter the piazza. San Gimignano is known for its many towers within and along the walled boundaries. In the Piazza del Cisterna is the Tower of the Devil. There are still fourteen towers remaining out of the original seventy-two.

When you are in the Piazza del Cisterna, go to your left to the Piazza del Duomo. The Duomo or Collegiate Church is worth seeing because of the beautiful frescoes, sculptures, and wooden statues. Right across from the Duomo is the Palazzo del Podesta built in 1249. You enter the palace through a vault called the Loggia. In this piazza are seven of the fourteen towers. The Torre Grossa is the tallest tower at 200 feet. You can tour the tower and the Pinacoteca Civica, or the Palazzo Nuovo Modesta. I hear the tower is a treacherous climb!

We had a great lunch at Ristorante Enoteca II Castello with pappadelle sul cinghiale (wild boar) and many other typical Tuscan dishes matched by good Chianti in a romantic atmosphere of a twelfth century palace. It is close to the Cisterna Square. From the well, go right down Via Castello. They have a beautiful inner courtyard with a beautiful overhead skylight.

Lucca

On a one-day trip, you can take the train to Pisa and then to Lucca if you want to combine the trips. In addition, a train goes directly to Lucca from Florence. Train #3052 leaves at 9:08 AM and arrives at 10:30 AM. Trains run about every 30 minutes so you can leave whenever you want. I like to get home before dark, so I would take the 5:32 PM arriving back in Florence at 6:52 PM. You can get your tickets beforehand. You will not need your Eurail pass for this short ride.

Lucca is a little city northwest of Florence. It was spelled Luca originally. Luca means illuminated glade. It is located near the River Serchio, a marshland. The Romans built a colony here in 180 A.D. They designed the colony with a forum and an amphitheater. It became an important duchy in the early middle ages. It also became the capital of Tosca. Pilgrims used Lucca as a resting place on their route to Rome. Lucca is famous for the immense wall around the city that is now used for bicycling and walking. Many churches and towers give the city a distinctive outline. Its fortress appearance protected it from attacks by the Pisans, their enemies.

The Signori ruled Lucca in 1400 under the governor, Guinigi. Under his rule, Lucca flourished and became known for its social and cultural achievements. When his wife, Ilaria del Caretto, died, he constructed a tomb with a memorial figure. The sculpture is of Ilaria in her bridal dress with a little dog at her feet symbolizing fidelity. It is now in the Duomo of Saint Martin. He began the construction of the city walls. They were not finished until 1645. Even later, under the rule of the Bourbons, they changed the walls into the park-like setting they are today.

When you arrive at the train station in Lucca, walk out to the front yard. You will see a path going into the city. If you take this path, you will end up inside the wall and it can be confusing. I prefer to go to the main entrance, San Pietro Gate. Go left down Viale Regione Margherita and make the first right leading to the main gate. When you pass through the main gate, the street splits around a little park. Take the left route and then go right onto San Girolamo. This street will take you to the large Piazza Napoleone. Napoleon created this piazza during the French occupation. His sister, Elisa Bonaparte Baciocchi, designed it in the style of the large squares in France. Here you will see some carriage rides that I highly recommend. The clip-clop of the horse down the cobblestone streets is quite entertaining. You will get a tour of the whole city that otherwise would involve a lot of walking. The cost was 60 Euros, worth every penny!

Enjoy a carriage ride in Lucca

San Michele in Foro

Afterwards, I recommend walking up the street lined with big trees, Via Vittorio Veneto. There are many little shops and cafes along the way and you will end up in Piazza San Michele. An outdoor market here usually provides some kind of entertainment. The day we were there, an organ grinder played his organ while a little monkey held out his cap for donations. You can also visit the church, San Michele in Foro. Lucca's Roman Forum once stood here. Faces of famous Italian patriots, including King Vittorio Emanuele, decorate the building. Between the arches, you will see sculptures of medieval figures. It is an amazing sight with intricate detail and carved stone. Saint Michele stands on top with spread wings protecting Lucca. The wings are hinged and they flap during festivals or during high winds. The facade is much higher than the rest of the church because they ran out of money when building the church. It was built around 1100 A.D. It is a little dark inside but there are some beautiful pieces of art. There is a wonderful pasticcerria (pastry shop) on Via Beccaria called Pinelli Pasticceri. Their cream puffs are remarkable! Via Beccaria runs parallel to Via Vittorio Veneto and begins at the southwest corner of the Piazza San Michele.

Giacomo Puccini's House

The street named Corte de San Lorenzo in the front of the church will lead you to a little piazza where you will find a statue of Puccini and the house where he was born. It is now a museum. Giacomo Puccini, who lived 1858-1924, became famous for the operas: La Boheme, Tosca, and Madame Butterfly.

Basilica de Frediano

In Piazza San Michele, the church sits on the north side of the piazza. On the south side, Via Roma goes to Via Fillungo. Turn left, going north again, and after going several blocks, when the street curves left, you will find the Basilica de Frediano, built 1112-1147. It is named after a fifth century monk, Frediano, who became the Bishop. Its golden mosaic high on the facade attracts onlookers. The mosaic depicts Christ and two angels with the Twelve Apostles below. The inside is beautiful with chapels and frescoes. By the entrance, you will see a huge twelfth century baptismal font decorated with scenes from the Bible. They have dedicated one of the chapels to St. Zita, Lucca's patron saint. Her mummified body is preserved here. Admission is free.

Piazza dell'Anfiteatro

Nearby the Basilica de Frediano, off Via Fillungo, you will find the amphitheater. The Romans, under Emperor Claudius, built the amphitheater in the first century A.D. It originally could hold 40,000 spectators. In the Middle Ages, it became a plaza and remains today as the center of town. In some of the buildings around the Antiteatro, you can still see some of the remains of the Roman civilization.

Siena

Siena is a well-preserved medieval town just an hour south of Florence. It is located right in the heart of the wine region of Tuscany. Siena competed with Florence during the medieval times. You can imagine the magnificence of the culture and society of the Sieniese. The Etruscans founded Siena as a Roman colony at the time of the Emperor Augustus. Siena reached its most successful times between the years 1200 to 1500. They sided with the Ghibellines against the Guelfs of Florence. They formed the "Council of 24" at this time. Siena was defeated by Florence in 1255. Siena and Florence experienced many turbulent years. Finally in 1269, the "Council of Nine" replaced the "Council of 24" to rule the city. The "Council of Nine" ruled until 1355. Siena experienced its most tranquil period in the city's history and experienced a healthy economic and cultural revival. The Sienese built many new buildings like the Cathedral, the Baptistery, and the churches of St. Francis and St. Dominic along with the Palazzo Pubblico. Illustrious artists such as Simone Martini, the Lorenzettis, Duccio, and many others created the beautiful artworks of Siena. Today, you can see the results of their efforts and passion in the churches, palaces, and fortress. Siena had lost thousands of their population to the Black Plague and famine during this period. Conflict between the nobles and working class increased. In 1355, there was a revolt against the "Council of Nine." Later, the Medici family of Florence gained control of Siena.

Torre del Mangia in Siena

The best way to get to Siena is by SITA bus. The SITA bus station is just south of the Santa Maria Novella train station in Florence. Check the bus schedule the day before. The bus ride takes you through the beautiful Tuscan countryside with olive groves and vineyards. It arrives near the historical sites. If you take the train, you will arrive outside the city and have to walk up a rather big hill. The roundtrip bus fare will cost 6.8 Euros.

It is very easy to get lost in Siena because of the winding narrow streets. When you get off the bus, you will be in Piazza Gramsci. If you face the park across the street, you want to go to the far left following the buildings to go to Via Malavolti, which will lead you to the Piazza Matteotti. When you see a little church, walk past it to Pianigiani that leads into Banchi di Sopra. This will take you to Il Campo, the center of town. There are two main entrances. One is down a little to your right.

Il Campo

The piazza is called Il Campo. It is bowl-shaped and covered in red bricks laid in herringbone style. There are nine sections to the piazza representing the "Council of Nine." Cafes and shops surround the piazza. A good restaurant on the Il Campo is the La Birreria. We had a delicious lunch for twenty-three Euros each including fried olives, lasagna forno, bistecca miale (pork), and red wine.

If you prefer a picnic in the piazza, try Morbidi, outside Il Campo, a famous local delicatessen selling Tuscan salamis, local cheeses, various pâtés, and take-out pasta dishes. Nearby the delicatessen of Manganelli, Via di Citta, 63, sells cured meats, cheese, olive oil, panforte, and ricciarelli (an almond cookie covered in powdered sugar).

Torre del Mangia

Once inside Il Campo, you cannot miss the bell tower, Torre del Mangia. It is 102 meters high with 332 steps. For the physically fit, the panorama of the city is beautiful. At one time, there were over 100 towers in Siena, but most of them were destroyed later on for building materials.

Palazzo Pubblico

At the bottom end of the Il Campo you will see the Gothic-style Palazzo Pubblico towered over by the bell tower, Torre del Mangia. The Sienese Republic built it between 1250 and 1310 as their governmental seat. Next to the bell tower, one enters the Courtyard of the Podestà, a brick colonnade built in 1325. Above the arched columns, you will see the trifora (three-arched) windows. In here, you see a series of governors' coats of arms and a stone statue of the Mangia and the *Wolf that Feeds the Twins*, the work of Giovanni Turino. It is the symbol of Siena. From this courtyard, you can enter the Torre de Mangia and the Civic Museum (Museo Civico) on the first floor. Here you will observe some impressive frescoes that are symbols of the city. The enormous frescoes in the Sala del Mappamondo and the Sala della Pace are quite impressive. Frescoes from the nineteenth century that depict Italy's first king can also be found there.

Fonte Gaia

At the top of the plaza in front of the restaurants, you will see a beautiful fountain, Fonte Gaia. Water was conveyed to Il Campo through a master-conduit around 1342. The Sienese celebrated the event joyously. They built the fountain, appropriately named Fonte Gaia (Joyous Fountain), the following year (1343). The original fountain was replaced in 1419, and then again in 1858.

Il Duomo

When you leave Il Campo, look for the street Via Pellegrini. Keep to the left on Via del Fusari. Il Duomo, a black and white Gothic masterpiece, is a very impressive site. The people of Siena worked for over two hundred years to build it. They never finished it because of the Plague in 1348. It has many famous artworks starting with the Piccolomini Library. The library holds frescoes that tell the story of the life of Pope Pius II in elaborately illustrated books. The pulpit by Nicolo Pisano is unique. Do not miss the beautiful Bernini statue of Mary Magdalene hidden away in a niche. Especially interesting is the floor made of mosaics. Divided into fifty-two squares, the mosaic depicts biblical scenes including the Massacre of the Innocents. Matteo di Giovanni designed it in 1482. Near the cathedral, you will see the Santa Maria de Scala, a hospital used to treat pilgrims, the poor, and orphans. Also, in the same area, you will find the Museo dell'Opera with famous artworks.

You will enjoy a good pasticceria (bakery) inside the walls named Bini, located at Via Stalloreggi, 91-93, (Via Stalloreggi runs from the backside of the Duomo). From the church piazza take V.D. Capitano and turn right on Stalloreggi. It has out-of-this-world sweets, for breakfast, lunch, and dinner.

There are many other sights in Siena but seeing them would probably take you at least another day. The best thing about Siena is walking through the streets and strolling across Il Campo. Several churches are scattered throughout this area, but you will have the most fun wandering in and out of the many shops. They have beautiful ceramics, special Italian food items, leather goods, and olive wood trays, bottles, and cutting boards.

Livorno

The main reason we went to Livorno was to ride the boats on the canals. However, we arrived too late in the morning. They do not go out in the afternoon. They do go out again in the evening. The origins of present day Livorno date back to the fifteenth century. A small port called Liburna existed in Roman times, built from a natural cove, which was under the domination of Pisa for all of the Middle Ages. A 1017 document mentions the presence of a castle named Livorna.

In 1421, the small port, under the reign of Genoa, was sold to Florence. At that time, Florence was undergoing major expansion and needed an efficient outlet to the sea. From this time on, the Medici family ruled Livorno for more than three centuries. They transformed the small village into one of the most important ports of the Mediterranean. At the end of the sixteenth century, Francesco I assigned Buontalenti with the task of making Livorno a full-fledged city. Buontalenti designed it to house 20,000 people inside the walls with three hundred ships in the port.

In 1606, Ferdinand I presented Livorno with the "Constitution Livonian" that gave incentives and privileges to merchants from everywhere who moved to the city to work. Thus, the foreign communities, called Nazioni, flourished; they were primarily Jews, who lived here free from the humiliation of a ghetto, but also Greeks, Armenians, English, French, Dutch, Spaniards, Portuguese, Russians, Muslims, and Waldensians. Livorno was declared a free port where goods were completely exempt from taxes. In 1629, Ferdinando II had a new quarter built by Venetian masters that connected the twenty-three islands by bridges: this quarter is now called Venezia Nuova. The year, 1736, marked the end of the Medici dynasty and the rise of the Grand Dukes of Lorraine who were connected to Austria's Hapsburgs. The city began to expand outside the Medici walls, slowly losing its city-fortress appearance. The nineteenth century was the city's golden century, a time of a great development of the economy, arts, publishing, and culture. Livorno became part of the united Italy in 1860. Livorno was seriously damaged during the Second World War and is currently trying to recover its past role as a cultural and tourism leader.

We arrived in Livorno at the train station. We took a bus and got off at the Piazza del Michelangelo. It is a huge oval shaped piazza that is actually a large bridge. It was built above a section of canal that connects the old city to the new city. There was not much going on there. We had planned to ride the boats on the canals (Fossi Medicei) but by the time we found them, it was too late. They only go out in the morning and evening. The boat tour, with commentary, offers an interesting perspective of the city and takes you around the *Fosso Reale* (royal canal), past the *Fortezza Nuova* (new fortress), and right under the Piazza del Repubblica, previously called *Il Voltone* (big bridge). A fosso, in Italian, is a moat, and the main waterways that cross Livorno were originally the defensive moats around the old walls of the city. They later took on an important commercial role in the transportation of goods on barges from the big ships to the warehouses situated along the canals, especially in the Venezia Nuova quarter. Fortezza Nuova (New Fortress) is an impressive polygon fortress in stone and brick, built at the end of the nineteenth century. The fortress is completely surrounded by Medici canals and dominates the old working class district of Venezia Nuova. It is a beautiful example of a sixteenth century fortification with its underground passages, large vaulted halls, and walkways for the guards. In this area, you will see the Fortezza Vecchia (Old Fortress). Moats surround the area. Behind the Fortezza Vecchio you will find the church, San Ferdinando. The exterior looks unfinished, but the interior is splendid with its marble sculpture. It did not seem too impressive from the outside, but we were glad we did go in to see its beauty.

Venezia Nuova

The Livornese designed this charming quarter, filled with canals, islands, and bridges in the seventeenth century to house the mercantile class. They designed the network of streets and canals so that goods could be easily transported to and from the nearby port. The dwellings of the quarter perfectly met the trade and living needs, and concealed elegant buildings divided into apartments, which contained warehouses on the first floor. These buildings can be best seen in the centrally located Via Borra, one of the nicest streets of the city. Venezia Nuova was seriously damaged during the Second World War.

Terrazza Mascagni

The seaside promenade is still one of the prettiest areas of the city. There is a large piazza called Terrazza Mascagni. The winding promenade ends with the Terrazza Mascagni. It is tiled with black and white floor tile that resembles a huge chessboard. You have a beautiful view of the sea and a circular temple that once hosted concerts and cultural events. On the promenade, you will see palaces, gardens, and historic buildings that are part of the history of this city.

Montenero Funicular

The highlight of a trip to Livorno is the Montenero funicular railway built in 1908. Initially powered by steam, its engines turned to coal, diesel, and electricity before it went solar in the 1980s. Take the Number 2 bus from the promenade along the sea. The incline railway takes tourists and pilgrims to a religious shrine cut into the rocks above the coastal city. The Sanctuary of Montenero is dedicated to Our Lady of the Graces, the patron saint of Tuscany. It is famous for a gallery decorated with ex-voti mainly connected to stories of miraculous sea rescues. English Romantic poet and militant atheist, Percy Bysshe Shelley, drowned when his small boat went down in a storm off Livorno in 1822.

Cinque Terra

The Cinque Terra (five lands) is named for the five scenic villages along the Ligurian coast: Riomaggiore, Manarola, Corniglia, Vernazza, and Monterosso. The villages seem to hang off the cliffs that form the coast. They are noted for their colorful exteriors of pink and yellow. The inhabitants of the Cinque Terra have a long history of fighting against intruders from the sea. They all have lighthouses or towers from which they could spot approaching vessels and warn the inhabitants of the intruders. The people live by fishing, by raising vineyards, and, now today, by tourism. In the summer months, in particular, they are inundated with young people seeking the sunny rocky beaches perfect for diving and hiking the Cinque Terra path between the five villages.

View of a Cinque Terra Village

From Florence, you take a train to La Spezia, a very large, beautiful seaport. From there, you can take a regional train that stops at the Cinque Terra villages. However, though the view is beautiful, it is quite a walk up and down the steep hills to get to the center of the towns where you find the restaurants and shops. If you decide to ride the train between the towns, check the schedule carefully as not all trains stop at all of the villages. To see Corniglia, one of the towns, you have to either hike or take the train, as it does not have access to the water. Forty years ago, I would have enjoyed the diving and hiking, but now in the golden years, I have discovered a great way to visit the scenic villages and coast without hiking. The ferry! The ferry usually runs from Easter to the end of September depending on weather.

Ferry to the Cinque Terra Villages

To take the ferry, take the train from Florence to La Spezia. The train goes through Pisa. To get in a full day, we take the 6:10 AM train from Florence arriving in La Spezia at 8:46 AM. You can take a bus down the hill to the sea or walk to the pier. We walked down in about fifteen minutes. When you get to the sea front, you will see the ferry station. The ferries leave every hour. We take the ferry at 9:15 AM to Portovenere. It is a beautiful ride that takes about thirty minutes. The ferryboats are large and have two levels. We like to sit on the bottom level toward the back to watch the wake of the boat pull through the beautiful azure water. You have to disembark in Portovenere and catch the ferry that goes to the Cinque Terra towns. It is possible to visit four towns by ferry. In order to arrive back in Florence before 9:00 PM, we decided not to go to Monterosso. We arrived in Portovenere at 9:45 AM and left Portovenere at 10:00 AM. We arrived in Riomaggiore at 10:30 AM and left at 11:30 AM. We arrived in Manarola at 11:40 AM and left at 12:40 PM. We arrived in Vernazza at 12:55 PM and stayed until 3:15 PM (15:15 in Italian time). We had a nice lunch in an outdoor cafe and then strolled around the village for awhile. The narrow alleyways are called caruggi. The town of Vernazza faces into the water with its large open harbor, castle, and church. Vernazza was a Roman installation that was strategically important during the age of the Maritime Republics in Genoa. It was also famous for its carpenters. If you are up for walking, we suggest a walk in the village that is dominated by a watchtower and the castle remains. In the small square, overlooking the seaside, you will see the church of Santa Margherita di Antiochia.

When we left Vernazza, we stayed on the ferry until we reached Portovenere. In order to make the train at 5:41 PM in La Spezia arriving back in Florence at 8:03 PM (20:13), we took the bus from Portovoenere to La Spezia. It was a hilly but scenic ride. To catch the bus you have to walk up the hill on the south side of the port (not too bad!) and catch the bus up there. There is a kiosk to buy your bus ticket. In addition, the bus arrives at the train station in La Spezia so you do not have to walk back up the hill to the train station from the port in La Spezia.

If you decide to hike, the first and easiest trail is call Lover's Walk or *Via dell'Amore*. It goes from Riomaggiore to Manarola. In August 2001, the National Park of the Cinque Terre started some new initiatives for tourists. One such initiative is that a ticket is now needed in order to walk on the Via dell'Amore which is the first part of the Cinque Terra trail. Tickets are also needed for the electric buses that connect the parking lots to the centre of the villages and the Center of Naturalistic Observations of Guardiola Tower. When you are in your prime, this walk is an easy walk that offers magnificent views of the coastline. There is an entrance fee. As you enjoy a delightful and relaxing stroll, the magic and beauty of the Cinque Terra will start to overwhelm you. If you hike from Riomaggiore to Manarola, you can then take the ferry to Vernazza. You can also take a train from Vernazza up to Corniglia (not served by the ferry) and then take the train back to La Spezia. The terraced hills are covered with vineyards that remind visitors of Corniglia's famous wine produced here since the ancient times. In fact, the wine was so famous in ancient times that vases excavated at Pompeii boasted its virtues! It is the less frequented of the five towns. We prefer the ferry.

Portofino

Little Boats in the Bay at Portofino

Portofino is a nice day trip from Florence leaving the province of Tuscany to Liguria. You leave Florence at 7:55 AM and arrive in Santa Margherita at 11:04 AM. You have to change trains in La Spezia and then you have to go up and down stairs to get to the right binario (platform). They changed the platform as they often do and we had to run up and down the stairs again. It looked quite like a Chinese fire drill and, fortunately, we ended up laughing instead of crying.

When you arrive at Santa Margherita, you walk outside the train station and board a bus to Portofino. Buy your bus ticket in the little snack shop behind the train station. You can also walk down to the pier in Santa Margherita and take the ferry across the Bay of Tigullio. We chose to take the bus and return by ferry. If you are adventurous, you can also walk: it takes at least an hour to walk the hilly 3.75 miles. I think it would be better to take the ferry there and the bus ride home because when we took the ferry back to Santa Margherita, the buses did not run very regularly back up to the train station which is actually at the top of a big hill. We took a taxi instead for fifteen Euros, rather expensive for a short ride.

The lovely colorful hotels at Portofino

Portofino is a fishing village that grew up and became a port for luxurious yachts visited by the rich and famous. However, it retains the appearance of the olden days with its peach, rose, and lemon colored narrow buildings with shuttered windows. The picturesque harbor is lined with cafes and luxurious boutiques leading up narrow, cobbled lanes to hotels and residences. You can also walk up to the church of San Georgio and Castello Brown, an old fortress. The path then leads up to a lighthouse on the promontory. Of course, we decided to enjoy the harbor activities instead. We took our lunch with us to avoid the expensive cafes, but we did splurge on gelato. It is a good idea to line up for tickets to the ferry early to get a seat with a view because the ferries are usually crowded.

When we returned to Santa Margherita by ferry, we had a very nice, early dinner in an outdoor café on the harbor. It is very enjoyable to watch the fishing vessels come and go and to see other large yachts cruising the harbor. Santa Margherita lies between Cinque Terra and Genoa along what is called the Italian Riviera. I actually think Santa Margherita is a nicer port than Portofino, and I would not mind planning to spend a night there.

Upon our return to the Santa Margherita train station, we took the 6:22 PM train that arrived in Florence at 9:22 PM. (Buy your tickets at the Santa Maria Novella train station the day before).

Pisa

Pisa is located in western Tuscany. It is known throughout the world for its famous Leaning Tower, but there is so much more to Pisa than just this striking landmark. The city of Pisa began life as a seaside settlement around 3,000 years ago and was first laid out in the mid-eleventh century. Pisa has many wonderful, historical monuments and buildings dating back many hundreds of years. Much of Pisa has retained its medieval appearance. Pisa is also known for its excellent university, established in 1343. It has become one of Italy's top schools. There are a couple of tourist information offices in and around the city center of Pisa and these provide the latest information about tourist attractions, museums, events, festivals, travel, and sightseeing.

The Campo dei Miracoli in Pisa

In the northwest area of Pisa, four impressive buildings stand in gleaming white marble on an immense green lawn. These imposing structures are enormous and breathtaking. The Duomo (cathedral) was built almost 1,000 years ago. The cathedral's bell tower is better known as the Leaning Tower of Pisa. The circular Battistero (Baptistery) is the largest of its kind in the whole of Italy, and the Camposanto, also known as the Holy Field, is one of the most beautiful cemeteries in the world. This area of Pisa is known as the *Campo dei Miracoli* or the Field of Miracles.

The Pisa to Florence train is a regional train and therefore no seat reservations are available. Buy your ticket at the train station in Florence before you go. Before you get on the train, validate your ticket at a small yellow machine on the platform (you will see others doing this). Then, hop on and find a seat. The trains run almost every hour. One that I like is Train #3111 that leaves Florence at 8:27 AM and arrives in Pisa at 9:29 AM. The very early morning trains usually have a lot of commuters and school children.

When you arrive, look for the yellow colored buses in the background just across the Pisa Centrale Train Station. As soon as we exited the train station, we just moved to the other side of the road. It is there where you have to board the bus going to the Leaning Tower of Pisa. You will not miss the bus stop. There will be many passengers waiting for the bus. Bus number 3 takes barely ten minutes to reach the tower. You can walk, but it will take around twenty minutes and I think that is lengthy when you want to spend most of your time at the Piazza dei Miracoli.

CHAPTER 15:
Conclusion

I wrote this book to share with you how you can travel even in your Golden Years. You can use this book to plan your trip to Italy in a way that will be comfortable for you and fit your special needs. There are many ways to go to Italy. The most popular is to take a tour. Many of the people I know who have traveled by tour say that they hope they never see another church! Some rent a car and often are stressed out by the driving in Italy, particularly in the cities. The public transportation system in Italy is fabulous. I hope you will find this book useful in planning your trip to Italy. It shows you how you can travel without the constrictions and the expensive price of tours.

A Perfect Trip to Italy is the result of many, many hours of research and travel experience. By reading this book, you will save all of the time it takes to plan a trip to Italy. I have a Web site where you can contact me for any questions that may arise. I will also appreciate hearing about your adventures in Italy—the good and the bad!

In 2010, I will be returning to Italy. I will write Volume Two of A Perfect Trip to Italy when I return in October. This year we will be visiting Lake Como, Lake Maggiore, Verona, Rimini, Ravenna, San Marino, the Amalfi Coast, and Rome. I will again stay in the apartment in Florence for two weeks. There is so much to see and enjoy in my favorite city.

Arrivederci! Vederla presto!

APPENDIX 1:
Italian Food Vocabulary

Acciughe: anchovies
Aceto: vinegar
Aglio: garlic
Agnello: lamb
Agnolotti: crescent-shaped, meat-filled pasta
Agrodolce: sweet-and-sour
Amaretti: crunchy almond macaroons
Anatra: duck
Anguilla: eel
Aragosta: spiny lobster
Arrosto: roasted meat
Baccalá: dried salt cod
Bagna cauda: hot, savory dip for raw vegetables
Bierra: beer
Biscotti: cookies
Bistecca (alla fiorentina): charcoal-grilled T-bone steak (seasoned with pepper and olive oil)
Bolognese: pasta sauce with tomatoes and meat
Bresaola: air-dried spiced beef; usually thinly sliced, served with olive oil and lemon juice
Bruschetta: toasted garlic bread topped with tomatoes
Bucatini: hollow spaghetti
Calamari (calamaretti): (baby) squid
Calzone: stuffed pizza-dough turnover
Cannellini: white beans

Cappelletti: meat- or cheese-stuffed pasta ('little hats')
Carbonara: pasta sauce with ham, eggs, cream and grated cheese
Carciofi (alla giudia): (flattened and deep-fried baby) artichokes
Carpaccio: paper thin, raw beef (or other meats)
Cassata: ice cream bombe
Cavolfiore: cauliflower
Ceci: chickpeas
Cinghiale- wild boar
Cipolla: onion
Conchiglie: shell-shaped pasta
Coniglio: rabbit
Coppa: cured pork fillet encased in sausage skin
Costata: rib steak
Costoletta: (alla milanese): (breaded) veal chop
Cozze: mussels
Crespelle: crêpes
Crostata: tart
Fagioli: beans
Fagiolini: string beans
Farfalle: bow-tie pasta
Fegato: liver
Fegato alla veneziana: calf's liver sautéed with onions
Fichi: figs
Finocchio: fennel
Focaccia: crusty flat bread
Formaggio: cheese
Frittata: Italian omelet
Fritto misto: mixed fry of meats or fish
Frutti di mare: seafood (especially shellfish)
Funghi (trifolati): mushrooms (sautéed with garlic and parsley)
Fusilli: spiral-shaped pasta
Gamberi: shrimp
Gamberoni: prawns
Gelato: ice cream
Gnocchi: dumplings made of cheese (di ricotta), potatoes (di patate), cheese
    and spinach (verdi), or semolina (alla romana)
Grana: hard grating cheese
Granita: sweetened, flavored grated ice
Griglia: grilled
Insalata: salad
Involtini: stuffed meat or fish rolls

Lenticchie: lentils
Maccheroni: macaroni pasta
Manzo: beef
Mela: apple
Melanzana: eggplant
Minestra: soup; pasta course
Minestrone: vegetable soup
Mortadella: large, mild Bolognese pork sausage
Mozzarella di bufala: fresh cheese made from water-buffalo milk
Noce: walnut
Orecchiette: ear-shaped pasta
Osso buco: braised veal shanks
Ostriche: oysters
Pane: bread
Panettone: briochelike sweet bread
Panna: heavy cream
Pancetta: Italian bacon
Pappardelle: wide, flat pasta noodles
Pasticceria: pastry; pastry shop
Pasticcio: pie or mold of pasta, sauce and meat or fish
Patate: potatoes
Pecorino: hard sheep's-milk cheese
Penne: hollow, ribbed pasta
Peperoncini: tiny, hot peppers
Pepperoni: green, red or yellow sweet peppers
Pesca: peach
Pesce: fish
Pesce spada: swordfish
Pesto: cold pasta sauce of crushed basil, garlic, pine nuts, Parmesan cheese
   and olive oil
Piccata: thinly sliced meat with a lemon or Marsala sauce
Pignoli: pine nuts
Polenta: cornmeal porridge
Pollo: chicken
Polipo: octopus
Pomodoro: tomato
Porcini: prized wild mushrooms, known also as boletus
Prosciutto: air-dried ham
Ragú: meat sauce
Ricotta: fresh sheep's-milk cheese
Rigatoni: large, hollow ribbed pasta

Riso: rice

Risotto: braised rice with various savory items

Rucola: arugula

Salsa (verde): sauce (of parsley, capers, anchovies and lemon juice or vinegar)

Salsicce: fresh sausage

Saltimbocca: veal scallop with prosciutto and sage

Sarde: sardines

Semifreddo: frozen dessert, usually ice cream, with or without cake

Sgombro: mackerel

Sogliola: sole

Spiedino: brochette; grilled on a skewer

Spumone: light, foamy ice cream

Tartufi: truffles

Tiramisú: creamy dessert of rum-spiked cake and triple-crème Mascarpone cheese

Tonno: tuna

Torta: cake

Tortelli: pasta dumplings stuffed with greens and ricotta

Tortellini: ring-shaped dumplings stuffed with meat or cheese and served in broth or in a cream sauce

Trenette: thin noodles served with potatoes and pesto sauce

Trota: trout

Uovo (sodo): egg (hard-boiled)

Uva: grapes

Uva passa: raisins

Verdura: greens, vegetables

Vongole: clams

Appendix 2:
Useful Italian Phrases and Words

Good morning: Buon giorno
Good Evening: Buona sera
Good night: Buona notte (when you are turning in for the night)
Goodby: Arriverdici
Please: Per favore
Thank you: Grazie
You are welcome: Prego
Yes/No: Si/No
Excuse me: Scusi
I would like to: Vorrei
I do not understand: Non capisco
How much does it cost? Quanto costa?
Postcard: Cartolina
Stamp: Francobollo
Ticket: Biglietta
Hotel: albero

You can use these sentences substituting the main noun to change the meaning:
What time does the train leave? What time does the bus leave?
    A che ora parte il treno? A che ora parte il autobus?
Dobbiamo andare alla banca di convertire i nostri dollari a Euro:
    We have to go to the bank to convert our dollars to Euros
C'è un negozio di alimentari vicino da?
    Is there a grocery store near by?

Where can I buy a hair dryer?

    Dove posso comprare un asciugacapelli?

Partiremo il 28 settembre.

    We will be leaving on September 28

Lei ha il ghiaccio?

Do we have ice?

Appendix 3:
Coffee

Any Italian will tell you where to find the best espresso in their town or village. They may even argue over their choices with families and friends (as each person has their own criteria and strong opinion)!

This is a passionate subject. Italians firmly believe that no matter your status or means, you should always demand the best for yourself. You simply deserve the best. This attitude is certainly evident when it comes to their favorite beverage, the thick and frothy caffé.

These are terms you may use when ordering your coffee!

- Un caffé: This is the simplest way of ordering an espresso. You will get the house classic version of a single espresso. If you are not a fanatic about your espresso, this will do. In Italy, an espresso comes in a very small amount and is smooth, dark, creamy and delicious.
- Un caffé macchiato (spotted): This is a request for an espresso with a quick shot of frothy milk (in a much smaller amount than that found in a cappuccino).
- Un caffé corretto (corrected): This is more popular than you may think, especially among men. It is a request to "correct" the coffee with one's favorite aquavit or liquor of choice, such as "corretto al rum, corretto al cognac, corretto al ..." (you fill in the blanks).
- Un caffé basso (low): You are asking for a version of espresso that sits low in the cup (less water) and a stronger result.
- Un caffé ristretto (narrow or condensed): This is a condensed version of espresso with less water, essentially the same as a caffé basso (above).

- Un caffé alto (high): This version must appear higher in the cup than a regular espresso hence entails more water than a normal single espresso and is less strong.
- Un caffé lungo (long): This is the same as un caffé alto (above).
- Un caffé doppio (double): This is similar to what you can order in the U.S. It is the equivalent of two doses of espresso in one cup. A few of these double whammies and you will walk and talk a lot faster.
- Un caffé al vetro (in glass): You are ordering your espresso in a glass rather than in a ceramic tazzina (espresso cup). Some swear their caffe' tastes better this way.
- Un caffé in tazza grande (in a large cup): You prefer your tiny shot of coffee in a large cup. This is very trendy now.

Appendix 4:
Festivals in Florence

Carro Matto

This festival occurs the last weekend in September. Caro Matto means "crazy cart". A pair of white oxen pulls the cart. It carries over 1500 wine bottles (the traditional flask with straw bottoms). They are carefully assembled onto the cart and presented to the government in Piazza Vecchio. There is also a parade of marchers in historical costumes, drummers and flag throwers. The flag throwers perform in Piazza della Signoria.

It begins near Palagio di Parte Guelfa and heads to the Duomo. The religious authorities bless the wine. The cart proceeds down Via Calzaiuoli and stops at Chiesa di San Carlo dei Lombardi where an offering is made. It finally arrives at Piazza della Signoria around 5:00 PM. The flag throwers start their performances around 5:30 PM.

Rificolona

On September 7, children carry paper lanterns to celebrate the triumph of Florence over Siena in 1555. It also celebrates the nativity of the Virgin Mary or the feast of the Madonna. A boat parade illuminated with paper lanterns accompanies the procession. One myth is that the farmers would travel to Florence to celebrate the feast of the Madonna. As they traveled at night to get there at dawn, they carried primitive lanterns. The Florentines would ridicule them and shoot the lanterns with peashooters. That tradition still exists.

The Festa della Rificolona has, as part of its celebrations, parties in the square and street theater performances accompanied by their delicious traditional cuisine. The amazing festival ends with a long and color splashed procession from Piazza Santa Croce to Piazza Santissima Annunziata, which is led by the Cardinal. After a solemn address, the revelry goes on until the sun comes up. As one of the most important festivals, the organic food producers of Italy originally organized the procession. This tradition continues to this day.

Festival of St. John

The festival of St. John takes place in Florence every year on June 24. This Florentine festival is celebrated with medieval style football matches where almost anything goes while the crowd roars and makes merry while cheering on the players. In the evening, the center of the festivities moves to Michelangelo Square in the old city of Florence where they put on a marvelous fireworks display for the public.

Calcio

One of the most popular and well-known games is the Florence Calcio in Costume. It is a costumed football game played on June 16, June 24, and June 30 to commemorate the famous match of 1530. It is still played today by men in fifteenth century costumes. The soldiers in military encampments originally played to build up strength. Though calcio, in Italian, means football, the game as such bears no resemblance to football. In 1530, the Imperial army laid siege to Florence under the orders of Pope Clement the VII. The Florentines, to enact the siege, played the historic game on February 17, 1530 while musicians played from the roof of the Santa croce. The games have continued and are played until today on the three days that mark the day of the recurrence of the Patron Saint. The games are now played to tourists and spectators in colored costumes. Two teams of twenty-seven players play for an hour for the cheering crowds.

Scoppio del Carro

Scoppio del Carro, or the explosion of the carriage, is held every year in Florence on Easter Sunday. This festival signifies the Holy Fire that was kindled using the stone chippings from the Holy Sepulchre that was then used to kindle the flames on all the hearths in town. Every Easter Sunday in Florence, a great chariot dating back to the eighteenth century pulled by white oxen parades around the town from Porta a Prato to the Cathedral Square. A wire connects it to the main altar in the cathedral and when the time is right, during midday mass, the Cardinal Archbishop will light a rocket that is shaped like a dove with the Holy Fire obtained from chippings from the Sepulchre. The rocket would shoot down to the chariot that is filled with fireworks and would ignite with a bang to the cheers of the gathering. You can see the modern version on YouTube!

Festa del Grillo

The people of Florence believe that the song of the cricket brings luck. In late April or early May, the Festa del Grillo, or the cricket festival, is held. A market is held at the Cascine Park where crickets are sold in colorful, hand woven cages. According to tradition, if a man decorates his beloved's doors or windows with flowers and gives her a cricket, luck would favor him in love. On the days leading up to the festival, children hunt for crickets to cage them. The male crickets have a yellow stripe to make them discernible. Crickets that sing are believed to bring the household luck. The children would capture them in wicker baskets, take them to the park on the day of the festa, and release the crickets. The festival is held on the Sunday after Ascension Day.

Fall Harvests

The grape harvest takes place at the end of September all over Italy. The fields are full of people picking grapes. They fill up plastic containers, then carry them to the end of the row and dump them into a big open container that is pulled by a tractor. You see these containers full of grapes while you are driving down the country roads. It is quite a sight. You can even smell the fermenting taking place. This would be a great time to go to the Accidental Tourist cooking class.

The olive harvest takes place in November. Every meal in Italy involves olive oil. The extra virgin olive is produced from the first cold pressing. It is gold with a shade of green, very light, sweet and pungent. Across the countryside, you will see nets in red, green, and white stretched over the fields. Every day they grow heavy with olives as families and farmhands knock them into the nets. The harvest is a festival. You can visit olive estates throughout Tuscany in November.

The chestnut harvest takes place in October and November. Festivals are celebrated all across Italy. The nuts are used for eating and to make the chestnut flour. The chestnut is low in fat and calories, yet high in complex carbohydrates, oils, and vitamins B-1 and B-2. It is also the only nut to contain a significant amount of Vitamin C. They have twice as much starch as potatoes.

They grow in large, dense forests usually high in the mountains. After gathering the chestnuts, they still use the traditional method. They shovel them into the top of a two-story stone oven and build a fire on the bottom floor. They are slow roasted for several days. The most popular are the castagne and marroni.

APPENDIX 5:
Italian Recipes

Lasagna Bolognese

2 Tbs. butter
6 slices bacon, diced
½ lb. ham
1/4 lb. ground veal
1/4 lb. ground pork
1 lb. ground beef
1 ½ c. chopped onion
½ c. finely chopped carrots
½ c. finely chopped celery
¼ lb. sliced mushrooms
3 cloves garlic, mined
1 pinch ground cloves
¼ tsp ground nutmeg
3 Tbs. tomato paste
1 c. dry white wine
3 c. chicken stock
1 ½ tsp. salt
¼ tsp. black pepper
4 chicken livers, finely chopped
½ c. heavy cream
¼ cup chopped parsley
1 pkg. no-precook lasagna noodles
1 c. freshly grated Parmesan cheese

1. In a large pot, heat the butter over medium heat.

2. Add the bacon and ham and saute until caramelized and light brown, about 10 minutes

3. Add the ground meats and cook over high heat until well browned, stirring constantly, about 20 min.

4. Add the onion carrots, celery and mushrooms and cook until soft

5. Add the garlic, cloves and nutmeg to the pan and cook for 2 min.

6. Add tomato paste and cook for 2 min.

7. Add the wine and cook until almost evaporated.

8. Add stock and simmer over medium high heat until sauce is thickened and flavorful, about 45 min to 1 hour. Season with salt and pepper to taste.

10. Add the chicken livers to the pot and cook 5 min.

11. Stir in the cream and parsley.

12. Set aside until ready to assemble lasagna.

13. Preheat oven to 350 degrees

14. Butter a large rectangular baking dish, then spoon ½ c. meat sauce onto the bottom of the dish.

Bechamel Sauce
6 Tbs. butter
6 Tbs. flour
4 ½ c. milk
½ tsp. ground nutmeg

15. Make Bechamel sauce: In a saucepan, melt the butter over low heat and stir in flour, stirring constantly until smooth, about 2 min. Slowly whisk milk into the flour, stirring vigorously to blend together. Set over high heat and quickly bring to a boil for 1 min. stirring. Allow to cook another 5 min., or until floury taste is gone. Remove from heat and add salt and nutmeg to taste.

16. Cover meat sauce with lasagna.

17. Top the lasagna with a layer of meat sauce, completely covering, a layer of Bechamel and a light dusting of cheese.

18. Repeat layering lasagna, sauces, and cheese ending up with a topping of bechamel and cheese. Bake until the lasagna is bubbling and golden brown, about 1 hour. Allow to rest 10 min. before serving.

Pesto Sauce

4 to 4 ½ c. fresh basil leaves
1 c. extra virgin olive oil
4-6 Tbs. pine nuts
2/3 c. grated Parmesan cheese
Salt and pepper to taste

Combine all ingredients in container of food processor or blender and process.
Turn off and on until sauce is formed with small bits of basil still visible
To serve: blend 2-3 Tbs. of soft butter into freshly cooked pasta. Blend several
Tbs. of pesto sauce into pasta before serving. Divide remainder of sauce over
servings.

Pappa Al Pomodoro Soup
(Italian Tomato Bread Soup)

6 cloves garlic
1 large onion, peeled, cut in half, thinly sliced
1/4 cup olive oil
1/2 teaspoon red chili pepper
1 (1 3/4 lb) can plum tomatoes
1 lb stale bread, sliced, torn into small pieces
6 cups broth, of your choosing
1 cup packed basil, shredded
Grated Parmesan cheese
Extra virgin olive oil

Sauté the garlic and onion in olive oil with the chili pepper until the garlic has
lightly browned and the onion is just getting golden; add the tomatoes; season
with salt; add half the basil leaves torn into tiny pieces; crush the tomatoes
with the back of a wooden spoon and stir; cook until the tomatoes fall apart
(about 20 minutes). Put the bread into the sauce; the bread will soak up the
sauce and it will get quite thick; add enough stock to soften the bread and to
make it liquidy; add the remaining basil and cook until the bread becomes a
kind of mush (this is called 'pappa'). Serve, sprinkling with Parmesan cheese
and a drizzle of extra virgin olive oil over each serving.

Ricottta Al Forno (Baked Ricotta)

3 containers of 15-oz. ricotta cheese or 2 lbs. fresh ricotta
2 Tbs. butter or margarine, at room temperature
3 Tbs. bread crumbs
4 large eggs
1.2 c. grated Parmesan cheese
¾ c. pitted black olives, quartered
½ tsp. salt
Freshly ground pepper to taste
Italian parsley sprigs

Drain ricotta if watery by placing on large square of double-thickness cheesecloth. Gather two diagonally opposite corners and tie together, forming a ball of cheese. Tie the other two ends around faucet over kitchen sink. Drain cheese at least one hour. Heat oven to 350. Use the 2 Tbs. of butter to grease an 8-inch springform pan. Coat with breadcrumbs; shake out excess. Put ricotta, eggs, and Parmesan in a medium-size bowl; mix with a spoon until blended. Stir in olives. Season cautiously with salt and pepper, remembering olives and Parmesan are salty. Pour mixture into prepared springform pan. Bake one hour and 15 minutes or until top is firm and golden. Cool. Remove sides of pan, place pie with pan base on serving dish. Garnish with parsley. Makes 4 to 6 regular servings or 10 party-size servings.

Taramisu

3 Tbs. sugar
2 egg yolks
2 oz. cream
5-3/8 oz. mascarpone cheese
1 oz. Marsala wine
7 oz. heavy whipping cream
2 c. espresso or strong coffee
½ c. warm water
24 French style ladyfingers
3 Tbs. powdered cocoa

Prepare Cream Mixture
In an electric mixer, whip sugar and egg yolks on high speed until pale yellow

and thick. With mixer on medium speed, add cream and whip until smooth. Add mascarpone cheese and Marsala wine.

Mix until incorporated. Whip the cream and fold into the mixture. Refrigerate.

<u>Prepare Espresso Mixture</u>

Combine espresso, additional Marsala, sugar, and warm water.

<u>Assembly</u>

Dip ladyfingers in espresso mixture. Place one layer of dipped ladyfingers on bottom of serving platter. Top with one layer of cream mixture. Add another layer of dipped ladyfingers. Top with a second layer of cream mixture. Sift cocoa over top.

Sugo di Carne (Tomato meat sauce)

3 Tbs. extra-virgin olive oil
3 Tbs. butter
1 medium onion, finely diced
1 carrot, finely diced
1/2 stick celery, finely diced
1 garlic clove, diced
1/2 lb ground meat
1/4 cup dry white wine
Salt and pepper
2 1/2 cups tomatoes, puréed in a blender
Pinch of nutmeg
2 Tbs. milk or heavy cream

Place oil and butter in a saucepan, and turn the heat to medium.

When the butter starts foaming, add the diced onion, carrot, celery, and garlic. Sauté and stir until the onion is soft and translucent. Add the ground meat. Stir with a wooden spoon, and break the meat into small bits. Cook until the meat is fully browned.

Add the wine, salt, and pepper. Turn the heat to high, and let the wine evaporate, add the tomato, nutmeg, and milk. When the sauce starts boiling, turn the heat to low. Cover the saucepan and simmer slowly for about 1 hour, stirring occasionally.

Gnocchi

Fill a stockpot three quarters full with water, bring to a boil, and add salt. When the water is at a fast boil, drop the gnocchi in a few at a time to avoid damaging them. The gnocchi will fall to the bottom of the pot

In a skillet large enough to contain the gnocchi, place the butter and sage leaves. Turn heat to medium to melt the butter. After about 1 to 2 minutes, the gnocchi will come up to the surface, and this will be the sign that they are cooked. Do not drain gnocchi in a colander like the one you would do with pasta. Gnocchi are very soft and may be damaged. Instead, remove them as soon as they float to the surface, with the help of a large slotted spoon or strainer, draining thoroughly. Transfer the gnocchi to the skillet and sauté briefly, stirring gently with a large spoon, until the gnocchi are fully covered by the butter. Transfer to a serving dish, top with the grated Parmigiano cheese.
Serve hot at once,

Risotto Con Funghi Porcini Secchi (Risotto with Dry Porcini Mushrooms)

1 oz. dry porcini mushrooms, soak in warm water for 1 hour or until soft

1-2 cups fresh quartered button or sliced white mushrooms (if you use canned, use straw)
5 cups (approximately 1 liter) broth, warm to a simmer in a small saucepan
3 Tbs. extra-virgin olive oil
3 + 2 Tbs. butter
1 medium onion, finely chopped
1 garlic clove, finely diced
1 bunch Italian parsley, finely chopped
1 1/2 cups arborio rice
1/4 cup dries white wine
Salt and pepper
4 oz Parmigiano Reggiano cheese, freshly grated

In a saucepan, put the extra-virgin olive oil and 3 tablespoons of butter. Turn heat to medium. When the butter starts foaming, add the onion and garlic, and sauté until the onion becomes soft. Add the mushrooms (reserving the water and half of the parsley) and sauté for few minutes. Add the rice and stir for about 2 minutes until well coated. Add the wine and stir to evaporate it. Add ¼ cup broth, and salt and pepper. Stir to prevent the rice from sticking to the pan. When the rice begins absorbing the liquid, add more broth. Repeat this step of adding the broth and stirring, keeping the rice at the consistency of a dense paste. Also, stir in half of the mushroom soaking water. After about 18 minutes, stir in the Parmigiano Reggiano cheese, and 2 tablespoons butter. Continue stirring and adding a small quantity of broth. The rice will be ready in about two more minutes, when al dente (firm but not too soft or overcooked). Cooking time may vary. When the risotto is ready, top with the rest of the chopped parsley. Serve at once.

Chicken Marsala
(serves 2)

2 boneless, skinless chicken breasts, pounded thin
flour, spread on a plate
1/4 cup olive oil
1/2 pound of mushrooms
1/2 cup Marsala wine
2 Tbs. butter
1/2 cup chicken broth
Salt and Pepper to taste

Heat olive oil in large sauté pan over medium-high heat
When the oil is hot, dredge both sides of the chicken breasts in flour, shake off excess flour, and place in pan. Sauté chicken, turning once, until lightly browned on both sides. Transfer the chicken to a warm plate. Drain all but a little bit of the oil and add mushrooms. Sauté the mushrooms until they begin to release their juices.

Add the Marsala wine, and scrape loose with a wooden spoon all browning residues on the bottom and sides of the pan. Add butter, chicken broth, salt and pepper. Cook until the liquid is reduced by half, approximately 5 minutes. Place the chicken breasts back in the pan and cook until heated through. Transfer the chicken breasts to warm serving plates; pour sauce over them and serve.

APPENDIX 6:
Sample Itinerary

September 1	Arrive	
September 2	Florence	Get settled
September 3	Florence	Duomo
September 4	Florence	Uffizi
September 5	Venice	Hotel Delfino
September 6	Venice	Gondola ride
September 7	Florence	Oltrano - Pitti, Boboli
September 8	Florence	Piazza Repubblica
September 9	Rome	Limo tour
September 10	Florence	Shopping
September 11	Siena	By SITA bus
September 12	Florence	San Lorenzo
September 13	Cinque Terra	Ferry
September 14	Florence	Santa Croce
September 15	Florence	San Marco
September 16	Portofino	Santa Margherita
September 17	Florence	Piazza della Signoria
September 18	San Gimignano	By SITA bus
September 19	Livorno	By train
September 20	Florence	Cooking class
September 21	Lucca and Pisa	By train

September 22	Florence	Piazza Michelangelo
September 23	Florence	Shopping/Fiesole
September 24	Florence	Medici Villas- limo
September 25	Milan	By train, Hotel Novotel
September 26	Milan	Last Supper
September 27	Leave	

APPENDIX 7:
Sample Packing List

PACKING LIST				
CARRYON/WITH WHEELS	**TRAVEL BAG**	**WAISTPACK**	**BUY THERE**	**WEAR**
	c-pap, mask, hose	adapters	curling iron	
3 pants, lightweight, easy dry	make-up	camera	shampoo	black jacket
2 lightweight jackets	eyeliner	camera cards	rinse	black pants
5 tops	shampoo-small	camera cords	bar soap	b & w top
shawl	rinse-small	cell phones	deodorant	compression socks
3 scarves	hairspray-small	cell phone cords	toothpaste	watch
2 nightgowns	deodorant- small	batteries	insect repellent	neck pillow
lightweight robe	small toothpaste	video camcorder	tissue & tp	
sandals/slippers	small bar soap	camcorder cards	sketch pad	
2 comfortable shoes,	Vitamins	camcorder cords	CD Italian	
thick-soled	medications	reading glasses	water	
7 sets underwear	shower cap	bottle holder	ice	
socks regular	razor	eyeglasses	coffee	
raincoat	aspirin	MP3 player/cords	creamer	
umbrella	Ammodium AD		food	
colored pencils/pastels	Airborne	**NECK POUCH**	tea	
journal	Benedryl-to sleep	plane tickets		
address books	tweezers	Eurailpass		
copies of tickets,	nailclippers	passport		
vouchers/reservations	first aid kit/bandaids	Dr. License		
small dictionary	alarm clock	credit card		
photos	pens	debit card		
washcloths	Qtips			
	hairbrush/comb			
	tissues-sm pkgs			
	wipes			
	snacks			
	tictacs/mints/gum			
	crossword			
	paperback			
	A Perfect Trip to Italy			
	name/business cards